The Titfield Thunderbolt

A play

Philip Goulding

Based on the original Ealing comedy screenplay by T.E.B.Clarke

Samuel French — London
www.samuelfrench-london.co.uk

ISBN 978-0-573-01441-0

www.samuelfrench.co.uk
www.samuelfrench.com

For Amateur Production Enquiries

United Kingdom and World excluding North America
plays@SamuelFrench-London.co.uk
020 7255 4302/01

Each title is subject to availability from Samuel French, depending upon country of performance.

THE TITFIELD THUNDERBOLT

First presented by New Perspectives Theatre Company, in December 1997 to February 1998, with the following cast:

Clifton/Joan Weech/Miss Coggett	Catherine Neal
Mr Blakeworth/Sam Weech	Graham Colclough
Mr Valentine/Vernon Crump/ Mr Clegg	Michael Strobel
Lady Edna Chesterford	Mary Elliot Nelson
Dan/Harry Crump/Mr Ruddock/ Mrs Bottomley/Sergeant Wilson	John Davitt

Directed by Gavin Stride
Designed by Alison Hefferman

Subsequently presented by Third Space in Farnham, Surrey, from Cotober to December 2004, with the following cast:

Clifton/Joan Weech/Miss Coggett	Sarah Lawrie
Mr Blakeworth/Sam Weech	Clive Holland
Mr Valentine/Vernon Crump/ Mr Clegg	Michael Strobel
Lady Edna Chesterford	Francine Morgan
Dan/Harry Crump/Mr Ruddock/ Mrs Bottomley/Sergeant Wilson	Edmund Wood

Directed by Gavin Stride
Designed by Iain White

Subsequently presented in a co-production by Bill Kenwright and CV Productions at the Queen's Theatre, Hornchurch, and Windsor Theatre Royal, from August to October 2005, with the following cast:

Clifton/Joan Weech/Miss Coggett	Loveday Smith
Mr Blakeworth/Sam Weech	Steven Pinder
Mr Valentine/Vernon Crump/ Mr Clegg	Paul Leonard
Lady Edna Chesterford	Kate O'Mara
Dan/Harry Crump/Mr Ruddock/ Mrs Bottomley/Sergeant Wilson	Philip Reed

Directed by Bob Carlton
Designed by Rodney Ford
Lighting designed by Chris Jaegar

COPYRIGHT INFORMATION

(See also page ii)

CHARACTERS

Lady Edna Chesterford
Clifton
Mr Blakeworth
Dan Taylor
Vernon Crump
Harry Crump
Joan Weech
Sam Weech
Mr Valentine
Miss Coggett
Mr Ruddock
Mrs Bottomley
Sergeant Wilson
Mr Clegg

Suggested doubling for a cast of 5

ACTOR 1 (F):
Clifton/Joan Weech/Miss Coggett
ACTOR 2 (M):
Mr Blakeworth/Sam Weech
ACTOR 3 (M):
Mr Valentine/Vernon Crump/Mr Clegg
ACTOR 4 (F):
Lady Edna Chesterford
ACTOR 5 (M):
Dan/Harry Crump/Mr Ruddock/Mrs Bottomley/ Sergeant Wilson

COPYRIGHT MUSIC

The notice printed below on behalf of the Performing Right Society should be carefully read if any copyright music is used in this play.

The permission of the owner of the performing rights in copyright music must be obtained before any public performance may be given, whether in conjunction with a play or sketch or otherwise, and this permissionis just as necessary for amateur performances as for perfessional. The majority of copyright musical works (other than oratorios, musical plays and similar dramatico-musical works) are controlled in the British Commonwealth by the Performing Right Society Ltd, 29-33 Berners Street, London W1P 4AA.

The Society's practice is to issue licences authorizing the use of its repertoire to the proprietors of premises at which music is publicly performed, or, alternatively, to the organizers of musical entertainments, but the Society does not require payment of fees by performers as such. Producers or promoters of plays, sketches, etc., at which music is to be performed, during or after the play or sketch, should ascertain whether the premises at which their performances are to be given are covered by a licence issued by the Society, and if they are not, should make application to the Society for particulars as to the fee payable.

A separate and additional licence from Phonographic Performances Ltd, 1 Upper James Street, London W1F 9DE, is needed whenever commercial recordings are used.

Please note that an enlarged version of the song
which appears at the back of this script –
The Ferroequinologist's Lament № 6.
composed by Alan Edward Williams –
is available on free loan from Samuel French Ltd.

FIREARMS NOTICE

With regards to the rules and regulations of firearms and other weapons used in theatre productions, we recommend that you read the Entertainment Information Sheet No. 20 (Health and Safety Executive).

This information sheet is one of a series produced in consultation with the Joint Advisory Committee for Broadcasting and the Performing Arts. It gives guidance on the management of weapons that are part of a production, including firearms, replicas and deactivated weapons.

This sheet may be downloaded from: www.hse.gov.uk. Alternatively, you can contact HSE Books, P O Box 1999, Sudbury, Suffolk, CO10 2WA Tel: 01787 881165 Fax: 01787 313995.

SYNOPSIS OF SCENES

ACT I

Scene 1
Scene 2 Titfield Railway Station
Scene 3 Down Country Lanes/Mungo's Farmyard
Scene 4 Titfield Railway Station
Scene 5 The Vicarage
Scene 6 *The Pig and Whistle* Public House
Scene 7 Titfield Railway Station
Scene 8 The Village Hall
Scene 9 Titfield Railway Station/On the Train/
On the Bus

ACT II

Scene 1 In the Countryside
Scene 2 On the Train
Scene 3 *The Pig and Whistle* Public House
Scene 4 Near the Engine Shed
Scene 5 The Vicarage
Scene 6 Titfield Railway Station/On the Train
Scene 7 Mallingford Station

Time - 1952

PRODUCTION NOTES

The Titfield Thunderbolt is a play about a small community. Wherever possible the audience should be a part of that community and the actors should get amongst them whenever they can. There is ample opportunity for this.

Alison Heffernan's splendid design for New Perspectives Theatre Company's 1997 small-scale tour of the play was an end-on affair. The main playing area was the raised railway station platform. When the characters boarded the train carriage they simply took one step downstage. To the left and right of the platform area were two higher, square rostra. The stage right rostrum functioned as the engine room of the train. The driver faced upstage whilst driving the train. The stage left rostrum functioned as the driving area of the bus. Other locations were suggested by minimal alterations to the main platform area. When the platform became the pub a pub sign appeared and the bench on the platform flipped over to become the bar. An old standard lamp and the picture of The Titfield Thunderbolt on the wall suggested the vicarage. A throw across the bench turned it into a sofa. It's preferable if these locations can appear swiftly - carrying heavy stuff on and off should be avoided wherever possible. The design should be ingenious and imaginative, making a virtue out of any financial limitations – using double-sided signs, clever carpentry etc. - and should, as much as possible, allow for a fluidity of movement from one scene to the next. In Alison's design there was a white picket fence at the back of the platform and then a narrow channel in between this fence and the painted rural landscape backdrop. When the train was moving the movement was suggested by trees, bushes, cows, horses, telegraph poles etc. flashing past. This was simply done by having actors run down the channel carrying small, amusing cut-out props. Photographs of Alison's design are available from the author.

The inspirations for Gavin Stride's 2004 production for Third Space included the Indian scientist and toymaker Arvin Gupta and the profusion of *Crafty Things To Do* manuals from the 1950s. Iain White's traverse design put the acting area down the middle of the space with the audience on two sides, facing each other. There were identically-shaped raised rostra at either ends of the acting space. These could represent pub, vicarage, platform, bus cab, engine room etc. by similar simple changes as in the New Perspectives design. These sections were movable (on wheels) so that they could be moved to the middle of the acting space and joined together to form the train and the carriage - and uncoupled when necessary so that the one could drift away from the other. There were special hanging devices over both sections so that pub signs, pictures, signals etc could be swiftly affixed to show the audience where the scenes were taking place. The Titfield Thunderbolt was cleverly constructed in this production from found objects such as dustbins, buckets, watering cans, oil drums etc. The idea was to capture a sort of "make do and mend" spirit - and this worked admirably.

In contrast, in the production at the Queen's Theatre, Hornchurch (designed by Rodney Ford) - a full-size engine came steaming on for the final scene. This was undeniably impressive – and if you have the financial wherewithal and the space to create such a spectacle – then go for it. But, if not, the main thing is to be imaginative – and to have fun.

Finally, a note on cast size. The play was written to be performed by a cast of 5 (2 women and 3 men). But if you have the players available the cast needn't be limited to that number. Weech and Blakeworth needn't be doubled, but if they are played by different actors certain doubling jokes will need to be cut. The characters of Valentine, Dan, Clegg, Ruddock and Miss Coggett would all make meaty enough individual roles if the company have the forces required. In fact, the only characters which should always be doubled are Harry Crump and Sergeant Wilson - the reason being that it's Wilson's resemblance to Harry which makes Joan realize she might possibly be in little bit in love with the younger Crump.

ACT I

Scene 1

The cast enter and sing The Ferroequinologist's Lament № 6. *The song can be accompanied by piano – or played on whatever instruments cast members are adept with – or even sung* a cappella

All At Adlestrop and Ampleforth,
Leaves lie on the line
At Cockermouth for Buttermere,
At Luton Hoo and Swine
The train is late at Bassenthwaite,
At Oyne and Auchmacoy,
Holmfirth and Hay-on-Wye,
Haydock - Ide, Knock - and Hoy

Oswestry, Usk, Mangotsfield,
Blyth, Bottisham and Lode
Now no trains go – from Edwinstowe
Or from Clackmannan Road
At Ullesthorpe and Lutterworth,
Pant, Parsley Hay and Brock
At Thornton for Cleveleys
No-one waits – and no-one winds the clock

From Billingb'rough and Horbling,
Claypole and Commondyke,
From Daisy Bank and Bradley
And Irlams o' th' Height
From Ecclefechan, Limpley Stoke,
From Box and Bamfurlong,
Audenshaw, Burra Tor,
Banff, Bovey - Birkenshaw and Tong

From Brampford Speke and Bluntisham,
From Gresford Halt (for Llay),
From Diggle, Delph and Saddleworth,
From Nigg and Gaminglay

From Campsie Glen, Heckmondwike Spen,
From Shap and Abbeydore,
Plympton and Pimlico,
Stockbridge and Spooner Row,
Kelso and Westward Ho!
Oh, we shall go,
We shall go no more.

All the cast remain on stage

As Edna introduces the characters, the actors might put on the relevant hat and step forward to adopt (for a brief moment) a dramatic attitude for that character. Some music under this, if possible – giving the flavour of an early radio play, perhaps

Edna Ladies and gentlemen, (Insert company name) Players proudly present *The Titfield Thunderbolt* by T.E.B. Clarke, in an exciting new adaptation by Philip Goulding. Starring (Insert name) as the Reverend Sam Weech — and the town clerk - Mr Blakeworth; and (Insert name) as Miss Joan Weech — and young Clifton. Also starring (Insert name) as Mr Valentine — and Mr Clegg — and Mr Vernon Crump. With a guest appearance by (Insert name) as Lady Edna Chesterford; and introducing (Insert name) as Mr Dan Taylor — and Mr Harry Crump — and Mr Ruddock — and Sergeant Wilson — and *(checking her cast list)* — Mrs Bottomley? Other parts are played by members of the cast. So, all aboard for the Titfield Thunderbolt!

Scene 2
Titfield Railway Station

It is morning. The station calendar on the wall tells us that it is Friday 6th June, 1952

Clifton, the Platform Manager enters, going about his duties — eventually putting up a poster telling of the closure of the line

Blakeworth, the town clerk enters and takes off his cycle clips

Dan, a scruffy old fellow, enters carrying a sack that he seems anxious to conceal

Blakeworth decides he'll try to make conversation with Dan

Dan blows his nose in his shirt sleeve

Blakeworth (*cheerily*) Morning Dan.
Dan (*reluctantly*) Aye.
Blakeworth Off to market with your spoils then, Dan? Sack looks a bit empty to me.
Dan What is or ain't in ere's my business and my business alone, Mr Blakeworth.
Blakeworth Quite.

Clifton walks past them on his way to put the poster up

Clifton (*to Dan*) Morning.
Dan Morning.
Clifton (*to Blakeworth*) Morning.
Blakeworth (*to Clifton*) Morning. (*To Dan*) Must be a bit of a home from home for you though, this place I reckon. How are things "Chez Dan"?
Dan You might seek to mock, Mr Blakeworth, but it do have its benefits, does living in a disused railway carriage.
Blakeworth Really? Perhaps you might care to elucidate?
Dan What? Well — as you knows, I likes a drink.
Blakeworth We'll encounter no divergence of opinion there, Dan.
Dan Ah. Well, fact is, no matter how much grog I might sup of an evening, I knows when I wend me weary way, I ent likely to put me key in the wrong front door. See, unlike these rabbit-'utches yon council puts up, my home has character. It's hindividual. And there's the rub. I've never yet unwittingly stumbled across another man's threshold, nor am I likely too.
Blakeworth I'm sure we'll all sleep sounder for being cognisant of that.
Dan 'Sides, I had many happy years working on these here railways, and now I spends me final days surrounded by me memories. Here comes the train then, Mr Blakeworth, I think I'll go further down the platform, I likes to bag me usual seat up near the engine.

He moves along and exits

The train comes in. (Noise of this can be voiced by cast). Clifton could wave the train in as it comes to a halt — there need not be any visible evidence of the train

Clifton Titfield, this is Titfield. All change. All change at Titfield!

Blakeworth attempts to make conversation with Clifton

Blakeworth Delightful morning.
Clifton (*pointing out the notice*) Not from where I'm standing, sir.

The notice says "Important Notice. The passenger train service between Titfield Station and Mallingford Junction will be permanently withdrawn on and from Saturday, the 21st June, 1952, and accordingly the public is hereby given notice of closure."

Blakeworth Oh dear. Ah well. Every cloud has a silver lining. No doubt we'll muddle along somehow. Chin up.
Clifton Thank you for your valuable reassurance, sir. The train is ready for boarding, sir.
Blakeworth I'll wait for Lady Chesterford if you don't mind. We like to share a carriage.
Clifton Suit yourself.

Vernon Crump enters. He gleefully eyes the sign

Vernon Lovely morning, Mr Blakeworth.
Blakeworth Crump. Surprised to see you out of your pit so early.
Vernon It's the early bird catches the worm, so they say. Thought I'd take a last look at the old place afore she passes into history.
Blakeworth There'll be those sorry to see her go.
Vernon Can't say as how I'll be one of 'em.
Clifton (*in Crump's ear*) All aboard now, for the eight forty-seven to Mallingford!
Crump I ent goin' nowhere.
Blakeworth Story of your life, eh Crump?
Crump I've a feeling the best days of my life are just beginning.
Clifton (*pointedly*) I said "All aboard!"
Blakeworth No need to resort to such vociferous declamation, man. Can't proceed yet, anyway. Lady C's still not materialized.

The following action takes place as they wait. There might be checking of watches, clocks etc. and looking around to see if Lady Edna has arrived yet. Perhaps this is a common occurrence — Lady Edna making the train with only seconds to spare

SCENE 3
Down Country Lanes / Mungo's Farmyard

The country lanes and the farmyard are located in any available space – aisles, the actual space in between rows of seats (don't worry about inconveniencing the audience, it's that type of show)

The chickens and any other creatures scattering in the barnyard can be voiced by the other actors

As this scene happens we see, simultaneously, the characters on the platform waiting for Edna to arrive

Harry Crump tootles along on his Steamroller

Up behind him steams Lady Edna Chesterford in her Morris Minor

(It is not expected that a producing theatre company will construct life size replicas of these vehicles. A couple of steering wheels will suffice)

Edna hoots her horn at Harry

Edna Move that damned steamroller aside, Harry Crump, some of us have trains to catch.
Harry If I move her over any further Lady C, I'll be in the ditch.
Edna As good a place as any for a Crump, in my opinion.
Harry Well if you fancy it so much, try it yourself.

Harry swerves

Edna (*beeping her horn*) Blasted hooligan! Come on, man, I'm in a hurry!
Harry I've got her flat out as it is.
Edna Blood and sand! You force me to take a short cut through Mungo's farmyard.

Edna does so. This might take her through the audience. (Sounds of squawking chickens and miscellaneous farm animals from rest of cast)

Meanwhile...

Scene 4
Titfield Railway Station

Clifton (*checking his watch*) Can't wait no longer. We're three minutes late already.
Blakeworth Three and a half, to be exact. Where the devil's she got to this morning? I'm due in Court at half-past nine.
Vernon Helping put some other poor debtor behind bars, no doubt.
Blakeworth Your familiarity with my duties speaks volumes, Mr Crump.
Clifton Time to go now! Lady C or no bloomin Lady C!

Clifton blows his whistle

Blakeworth boards the train. (This can be achieved simply by having the actors take one step downstage)

Edna rushes on

Edna Hold that train!
Blakeworth About time too!
Edna What's the idea, leaving me behind on market day?
Clifton Four minutes late, Lady Chesterford, ma'am.
Edna Church clock says four minutes early.
Clifton British Railway's run by Greenwich, not Titfield time. (*He blows his whistle again*)
Edna As a point of fact my great-grandfather built this station for Titfield, not Greenwich! (*Boarding the train*) And I'd have been here a good deal earlier had it not been for that young buffoon Harry Crump, and his antiquated steamroller snarling up the country lanes. (*Out of the window, aimed at Vernon*) A chip off the old block that one, if I'm not mistaken.
Vernon And a good morning to you too, Lady C.

The train starts to move off

Note: Whenever trains are in motion the actors should behave accordingly – swaying and jolting to the rhythm of the ride. In addition – and depending on the design, of course – upstage (as if through the far-side windows of the train) we might see objects passing – telegraph poles, trees, bushes, cows, horses, sheep etc. These could speed up or slow down depending on what speed the train is supposed to be travelling at. This device should be used sensibly, of course, so as not to pull focus from whatever else is happening

Blakeworth You want to try getting on your bike, Edna, like the rest of us, of an a.m. Keep you healthy at the very least.
Edna The bicycle is a recreational tool, in my opinion, Blakeworth, and an antiquated one at that. Shall we move further up the train? I do like to be near the engine.

Edna begins to lead Blakeworth up the train — their progress will eventually take them off stage

During the following passage, the train, the passengers and Clifton vacate the stage, leaving Vernon alone on the platform

What was I saying? Oh yes. We must embrace the march of progress.
Blakeworth Talking of progress, Edna. You'll have seen the sign no doubt.
Edna What sign?
Blakeworth About the withdrawal of the railway line. They posted it up, this morning.

Edna and Blakeworth exit

Vernon proceeds to put up a new sign next to the other one, whistling as he works.

Harry enters during this, momentarily startling Vernon

Harry Up to no good as usual then, Dad?
Vernon All legal and above board this time son, believe you me.
Harry They say there's a first time for everything.
Vernon What's eating you? Had enough of that old steamroller already have we? I knew it wouldn't last. You should have listened to your old dad. The wind of change has been blowing in this direction, son. And I've had a sniff of it for some time.
Harry I've no idea what you're prattling on about, Father. But it was a shaping up to be a good day 'til Lady Muck nearly run me into the hedge. Thinks she owns Titfield, that one.
Vernon Ah. Well she'll be needing to think again before too long. Because there's about to be a new power in the land. See?

The poster is now up. It reads "Very Important Notice. An alternative passenger Omnibus Service will be operated by Crump and Son Road Transport Company (incorporating the Titfield Road Transport Company) servicing the area formerly covered by the railway."

Harry Only one problem with that, Dad. We ain't Crump and Son. Nor will we ever be. Not in a business sense any road.

Vernon hands Harry a photograph

Vernon Afore you says another word. What d'you reckon to her?
Harry (*after a pause*) It's a knackered old bus, Dad.
Vernon Ain't she a beaut? And I got her cheap. Years left in her yet though, son, take my word for it.
Harry Two things my mother said to me on her death bed ——
Vernon God rest her soul...
Harry One. Never take the old man's word for owt. And two, no matter how desperate you are, don't go into partnership with your father.
Vernon She could be a bitter woman, though I loved her none the less for that. But even she'd have seen that this is different. We can't lose, son.
Harry No offence, Dad, but leave me out of it.
Vernon You don't need to make a decision immediately, lad. Just let me keep the name, eh? Indulge your old man for appearance sake. And once I've proved to you this one's a winner, you can hop on board at your leisure.
Harry Like I said, Dad, I've already got a job.
Vernon A steamroller driver! When you could be an "omnibus operative".
Harry I intend to make a go of it, Dad. I've been asked to put in an estimate for levelling a footpath through Ravens Wood. If I get that I'll be set up for the next few months at least.
Vernon You want me to put in a word for you, son?
Harry (*too eagerly*) No thanks, Dad — I wanna stand on my own two feet, see.
Vernon Like father like son, eh boy. (*He hugs him*)
Harry Leave it out, Dad.
Vernon (*leading him out*) Not still mooning over that young lass at the vicarage are you?
Harry Get off! I dunno what you mean.
Vernon (*off — proudly, knowingly*) Like father, like son.

Scene 5
The Vicarage

With a minimum of fuss, we have been transported to the Vicarage, where Weech, the Vicar, is furtively reading a railway magazine. When his niece Joan enters, Weech hastily pretends to have been studying his bible

Joan I'll get off now shall I, Uncle?
Weech What's that? Have you organized the flower rota, my dear?
Joan Yes, Uncle. It's just that I said I'd cover the end of the evening shift at *The Pig and Whistle*. It's Mr Moffatt's evening off, and you know what Mr Valentine's like. He's liable to take the relief barman's instruction "See yourself out when you've finished" as an open invitation to camp on the floor of the snug.
Weech Oh my dear, I do wish you would heed my desires and cease your casual employment at that den of iniquity.
Joan It's really not so bad as you imagine uncle. Besides, I don't like to be beholden to you for everything. You were kind enough to offer me a home after my father was detained as a guest of his late majesty, it's only right I make the effort to bring a little money into the house.
Weech Bottom drawer, eh Joan, old thing?
Joan Uncle?
Weech I'm quite worldly enough to have noticed that Crump boy casting furtive glances towards the vicarage as he trundles past on that contraption of his.
Joan I'm sure Harold Crump's not what you might call an appropriate suitor, Uncle. Having the background he does.
Weech The sins of the father must be forgiven, my dear. As indeed will be the sins of your father, my own dear brother...should he be fortunate enough to outlive his spell in prison. No, young Harry Crump must be judged on his own merits. Don't you agree?
Joan I've no idea why we're having this discussion, Uncle.
Weech Have it your way, my dear. As I've a feeling you shall. Off you go then. I shall continue to contemplate this Sunday's sermon.
Joan (*not fooled*) Yes, Uncle.

The doorbell rings

Weech And send away whoever that might be. It's far too late for visitors.
Joan (*perhaps pulling aside a curtain*) It's Lady Chesterford, Uncle. She appears rather agitated.
Weech Oh dear. In that case you'd better send her in, Joan, forthwith.

Joan exits

Greetings off

Edna enters

Edna Hope I'm not interrupting anything important, Sam.
Weech Not at all, Edna, not at all. Just reacquainting myself with the wisdom of the Lord.
Edna (*not fooled*) It's actually the railway I've come to talk to you about.
Weech The railway! Well I never. How exciting.
Edna You've not heard the news, then?
Weech There's news! In Titfield! What an action-packed evening this is turning out to be.
Edna They're closing it down, Sam.
Weech The railway? Never.
Edna It's true, I'm afraid.
Weech But we're the oldest surviving branch line in the civilized world. (*Referring to a picture on the wall*) "The Titfield Thunderbolt", Edna. From these magnificent beginnings we have been witness to a glorious chapter in the history of steam. I can't believe we are now expected to simply turn the page and bid farewell to such a focus of local pride.
Edna They say my great-grandfather lost the will to live the day they took that old beauty out of service. But it's not just us, this is happening everywhere, Sam. They've even closed the Canterbury to Whitstable line.
Weech So I heard. Doubtless there weren't men of sufficient faith in Canterbury. But here — no, it's unthinkable.
Edna Quite frankly, I was hoping you'd see it this way. We have to fight it, Sam. No doubt about it.
Weech Quite so, Edna, quite so.
Edna It'd mean a virtual monopoly for Vernon Crump, you know, if this went through.
Weech What's Crump the Elder to do with this?
Edna He's bought a filthy old omnibus. He intends to run an alternative service.
Weech And I'll warrant it will be alternative if Old Crump's anything to do with it.
Edna It could be the end of Titfield as we know it.
Weech Good grief. Well, I must confess, I'm at a loss to know what to suggest.
Edna I was speaking to Blakeworth about this on the train this morning.
Weech Blakeworth? Refresh my memory.
Edna The town clerk.
Weech Got him! Carry on...
Edna Well, he said that the only solution would be to buy up the line.

Weech My dear Edna! But surely one can't buy a railway these days, not now they've all been nationalized.

Edna This is where Blakeworth's knowledge came in handy for once. He says that the Transport Act of 1947 only nationalized existing railways. So a new——

Weech Company formed now wouldn't come under the act! But still — surely there'd be hundreds of conditions to fulfil.

Edna On the contrary, if we were to get a light railway order, most of them wouldn't apply.

Weech So...?

Edna I'm afraid that's where Mr Blakeworth's flow of useful information dried up. I suspect he remembered his position as a town clerk and realized that innovative forward planning wasn't included in his job description.

Weech Ah...

Edna Which is why I've come to you. Knowing your interest in — and knowledge of — such matters. So, the question is: how do we go about getting a light railway order?

Weech Prayer!

Edna Sam...?

Weech Prayer to the Ministry of Transport. It's a legal term.

Edna But where would we get the staff? We'd need an engine crew, signalmen, platelayers. And the railways are already short-handed, having cut their staff levels to the bone. They'd never let anyone go.

Weech What about those who've already been laid off?

Edna They're a disillusioned lot, in the main. Their get-up-and-go's got up and went. We need fresh blood. Folk of enthusiasm — foresight — ambition.

Weech Then you've answered your question yourself.

Edna Sam?

Weech Good gracious, woman! You whose great-grandfather built the railway! Don't you see! The solution's plain as day. We must run the line ourselves!

Edna Good Lord! — You're right, you're right! By heavens! What a stroke of genius, Sam! We'll run the line ourselves!

Weech Of course I shall drive the engine.

Edna And I'll be the guard!

Weech (*heavenward*) I'm gonna drive the engine. Thank you, Lord!

Edna Wait a minute. Small problem. Where'll we get the money from? I'm stretched to the limit keeping the estate ticking over since Pop popped his clogs. Had to lay the gamekeeper off last week. Blowed if I know what he did, anyway. But I figured if it was something I knew nothing about, then it couldn't have been that important anyway.

Weech Ah? Mm. (*Thinking*) Got it! We'll raise the money. We'll organize a raffle, a jumble sale and a fête. We'll revive the flower show, have a flag day, and plan a mile of pennies! I could even stage my *Charley's Aunt* again! (*Striking a Charley's Aunt pose*)
Edna Hmm. With respect Sam, you've already done all that in aid of the Church Steeple Appeal. And how much have you raised so far..?
Weech Forty-nine pounds and three shillings. And six pence.
Edna And we need something in the region of ten thousand pounds.
Weech Good God!
Edna I don't think even He could help us out of this one. But there is one person who just might be able to...
Weech Before you say it, Edna, my dear disgraced brother insists that the whereabouts of his substantial proceeds from the sale of the original crown of thorns to that gullible American gentleman are a secret that will follow him to the grave.
Edna It wasn't your brother I was thinking of, but Mr Valentine.
Weech Mr Valentine! A godless fellow! Besides, he made his fortune from the distillation of intoxicating spirits. I'll hear no more of it!
Edna Sam...? A railway of our very own...?
Weech Could he be persuaded, do you think?
Edna Let's put it this way — he's spent the last forty years standing folk drinks — what's to stop him standing us a railway?
Weech And where would we find Mr Valentine?
Edna Need you ask? The *Pig and Whistle* public house. If we get our skates on we might just make last orders.

Edna exits

Weech Public house eh? (*Heavenward*) May God forgive me.

Weech exits

Scene 6
The Pig and Whistle Public House

With the minimum of fuss we have been transported to The Pig and Whistle *public house, where Valentine is holding court, a large gin in his hand. Valentine has evidently been drinking for some time. Harry looks on. Joan works behind the bar*

Joan Last orders ladies and gentlemen please!
Valentine Another round for all those present, Joanie, when you're

ready. (*Pointing out member of the audience*) Except for that fellow there. Looks like he's had sufficient. Oh, and a large gin for me.

Joan You've already got one in your hand, Mr Valentine.

Valentine Well look at that. So I have. Joanie, Joanie, Joanie. As bright as a button. A star in our fernanernt — furry mint — sky, for heavens sake. (*Grabbing her*) I'm an old man, I grant you, Joan, but you can't fault my taste. And were I ten years younger, I'd win you. With gallantry and idolatry and — other trees too numerous too mention.

Harry Leave her go, Valentine, for goodness sake.

Valentine Who mentioned "goodness", man? I say — is she spoken for already, this rose of old England. Say it's not so, Joan!

Joan No she's not spoken for. But you can leave off anyway, thank you Mr Valentine.

Valentine Quite right. No offence intended, Miss Weech.

Joan None taken, Mr Valentine. (*To Harry*) And I'm quite capable of fighting my own battles, Harry Crump, thank you all the same.

Valentine Ladies and gentlemen, here's to our magnificent generals, General Gordon and General Booth. My mentors and my friends. Will you join me, young Crump, in drinking their health, and that of the lovely Joan, whose reputation you're intent on so gallantly defending.

Joan Harry?

Harry No thanks, Miss Weech. I'll not stick around where it seems I'm not wanted. Besides, some of us have work in the morning.

Harry exits

Weech and Edna enter

Valentine Whoops. Bit of a hiccup there on the road to contentment. Sorry if I queered the pitch.

Joan I've no idea what you're talking about, Mr Valentine.

Valentine You're not alone in that. Who's this? Odds bodkins, our good chaplain. I was just purchasing a round of drinks. Drinks for everybody! (*Of a member of the audience*) I thought she was barred. (*To Weech*) They'll let anyone in here you know. So what'll it be, your reverence?

Edna I think I should get these.

Valentine Wouldn't hear of it. I've staked me claim, ma'am. And I'll stand me ground and stand my round. You'll accept defeat like a gentleman, ma'am, or prepare to die — like a cur. Now, Mr Weech, sir, your pleasure if you please.

Weech That's most kind of you. Perhaps a small glass of sweet sherry.

Valentine Joan! A small glass of sweet sherry. That'll hit the spot eh, Lady Chesterford? And will it be the same for you? Or will you carry on as you were?

Edna (*attempting to avoid Weech realizing that this is not her first visit to the pub today*) Well — um — as this is the first of the day, I'm not sure what you——

Valentine Let us not quibble over the matter of the mere few empty hours that have lapsed since we last stood here together side by side. Mild and bitter, was it not? (*A sherry is passed to Weech*) Sup up, Reverend. Put some colour in your cheeks. You look very pale, don't you know.

Weech drains his sherry in one

Edna Mr Weech has just recently had a very nasty shock, Mr Valentine. You'll have um — heard that they're closing our railway?

Valentine Oh, my dear padre, all this time together and not one word of sympathy from me. You must think me a very cruel and unthinking old man.

Weech Oh — not at all.

Valentine But I insist!

Weech Actually — we, that is — Edna and I — were meaning to have a word with you about this railway business. You see — we're planning on taking it over — working it ourselves.

Valentine Well, what a stroke of luck!

Weech What's that?

Valentine I know just the man you need. (*Shouting*) Mr Taylor, sir. Mr Taylor! Joan, where's Mr Taylor?

Joan He's here, Mr Valentine.

Valentine Well, so he is.

Edna Of course, we need to find the capital…

Valentine (*not listening*) What you doing hiding up there, Mr Taylor? Stop dodging about, Sir, and come hither. You're going to drive an engine for these ladies and gentlemen.

Weech (*to himself*) Oh no.

Valentine Oh but yes, sir. Mr Taylor here's a railway servant of considerably long experience.

Dan Forty-one years.

Weech I'm aware of your service record, Dan. As a "platelayer".

Dan I can drive an engine!

Weech Puh!

Dan Better'n what you can.

Weech Then I daresay you'll be able to tell me at what percent of piston travel an engine cuts out before she starts her run.

Dan Eh?

Weech I rest my case.

Valentine First blood to the cloth, I'd say. But you'll not lie down without a fight, Mr Taylor. Come on man, have at him!

Dan What? Oh. Right. Then answer me this, your reverence: what's a samson?

Weech One surely doesn't require a knowledge of working slang to successfully operate a locomotive.

Dan I thought so. And no doubt you'll be a stranger to the petticoat pipe?

Valentine A hit for Mr Taylor, if I'm not mistaken.

Edna Come on, Sam – retaliate.

Weech What's the purpose of the firebox throat plate?

Dan When does an engine bark?

Weech What's a stuffing gland?

Dan How long's your jay rod?

Weech How do you free a clogged blower?

Dan How do you treat a big brass end?

Weech grabs him

Weech Will you answer my questions, man?

Dan Answer mine first! And take your hands off me while you're about it!

Joan Gentlemen, gentlemen! Order please! I'm surprised at you, Uncle. What sort of establishment do you think this is? And that's 'time' at the bar now. Time, ladies and gentlemen please! (*To the audience*) Come on, sup up, Madam. And you rabble, over there. Haven't you got homes to go to?

Valentine I declare the contest a draw. You must both drive the engine.

Dan Ah. Well, I'll believe that when I sees it. 'Night all. Miss Weech.

Joan 'Night, Mr Taylor. Straight home now, mind.

Dan leaves

Joan goes off at some point to tidy up in the other bar

Edna Dan's right, Mr Valentine. You see, this talk is all very well and good, but the plain fact is we need at least ten thousand pounds before we can even float our company.

Valentine Ten thousand pounds! Good heavens, Lady Chesterford! What's ten thousand pounds between friends?

Edna Nothing much to speak of?

Valentine Nothing much to speak of indeed. Money, my dear lady, is merely squiggles on paper. Symbols, nothing more. "I swear to pay the bearer on demand." Come along, ma'am. Let's drink to your success.

Edna Wait a minute — you mean — you'll finance us?

Valentine Me, ma'am? I say. What a charming offer. But come now, Lady Chesterford, what right have I to exploit your enterprise for gain? I, a weak and foolish old man——

Weech Rest assured, sir, you certainly won't gain by it.

Valentine — I, who already have enough for my few simple needs.

Weech You see, this line's been losing money for years——

Edna signals to him to shut up — he doesn't notice

—and it's bound to go on losing money.

Valentine Well here's an honest man. But for your timely warning I might have made a very foolish investment. Same again, Joan, my dear, for that fateful hour surely approaches when the infernal law decrees we're to drink no more.

Weech I think you'll find that fateful hour's been and gone, Mr Valentine.

Valentine Then whoever named the law an ass, knew well of what he spake.

Edna D'you know, I've just had a thought. Mr Valentine, what do you do in the mornings before *The Pig and Whistle* opens?

Valentine Why I do what any man of my kind would do. I patiently wait for the day to truly dawn.

Edna You mean — for licensing hours to commence?

Valentine Absolutely.

Edna Suppose the day could be made to dawn at thirteen minutes to nine?

Valentine Lady Chesterford, you're a poetess! A dreamer of beautiful dreams, no less! But alas, such a paradise could never exist, more's the pity.

Edna That's where you're wrong. There's nothing in law to prevent a railway company from opening a bar in one of its trains, whenever that train is underway. So — if you'd just agree to give us your backing, we'd promise to run a bar on the Titfield to Mallingford line every morning — and every afternoon.

Weech Excepting Sundays, of course.

Edna Of course.

Valentine You — you wouldn't tease an old man, would you, Lady Chesterford? Mr Weech? You surely wouldn't joke about such a sacred subject as this?

Weech As far as I understand the law, I assure you it would be quite, quite legal.
Edna You can write your own timetable.
Valentine In that case you, my very dear Lady, can write your own cheque!
Weech Alleluia!

Possibly music on tape here, if needed. Something that heralds the arrival of a new positivism. The function being to bridge the brief interlude as the next scene is set

Scene 7
Titfield Railway Station

With a minimum of fuss we are back at the station

The station calendar tells us it's Friday 13th June, 1952

Clifton enters, and to the ominous toll of a bell, sticks a notice on the wall saying "Titfield-Mallingford Railway, Ministry of Transport, inquiry will be held at the Village Hall, Titfield, Friday 13th June" then exits

Edna enters and paces impatiently

Weech enters with a newspaper

Edna Ah Sam, there you are.
Weech You wanted to see me, Edna.
Edna Yes. I've some news.
Weech Talking of which, you'll have seen *The Mallingford and District Bugle* I imagine.
Edna Oh I wouldn't worry too much about what that rag has to say.
Weech But they're making us look ridiculous. Have you seen this cartoon? "Victims of Amateuritis". It really is too embarrassing.
Edna Forget it, Sam, it's not important.
Weech But the truth of the matter is, Edna, that we are amateurs. There's no escaping the fact.
Edna Not for much longer, Sam. That's what I wanted to see you about. Dan's persuaded the present crew of the train from Titfield to Mallingford to let you ride in the engine with them over the next few days. It'll be like a course of proper lessons.
Weech Me! Ride in the engine! Really? I'm gonna ride in the engine!

Edna (*Ssshing him*) But it's just between us and them, you understand.
Weech Oh I see. Quite right too. Saints preserve us, I'm to ride in the engine. Well in that case, Edna, I really must press on with my duties.
Edna What d'you mean? You'll be present at the meeting?
Weech Impossible Edna, I'm afraid. I must make my rounds.
Edna Are you sure, Sam?
Weech Absolutely, Edna. I'm afraid even I can't be in two places at one time. And no matter how aspirational our ambitions might become, I'm still the vicar, remember. (*As he exits*) I'll try to pop by later.

Weech exits

Vernon and the glamorous Miss Coggett enter together

Vernon adds to the poster advertising his bus service a sticker proclaiming: "It's safer by bus"

Vernon Ain't she a beauty? I trust you found the journey here comfortable, Miss Coggett.
Coggett I've no complaints, thank you, Mr Crump.
Vernon Call me Vernon, Miss Coggett. When you've travelled in a man's omnibus, you're entitled to a degree of familiarity.
Coggett I prefer to keep things on a professional standing, if you don't mind, Mr Crump.
Crump I fully understand your reasoning, Miss Coggett, though you'll be aware no doubt, there are those round here to whom "professional" is a dirty word. Oh, I didn't see you there, Lady Chesterford. Good day to you. I trust the condemned woman ate a healthy breakfast before preparing to meet her Waterloo. Ah well, the end of an era. There's the train now coming in, Miss Coggett. Feast your eyes on it while you can, Lady C, it's a sight you'll see no more of come the end of next week.

The train pulls in

Ruddock gets off. He surveys the scene with contempt

Ruddock So. This is Titfield is it? Distinctly unimpressive, if you'll excuse me saying so. (*He notices Coggett, and is immediately attracted*) I say...! Hallo! Ruddock. Ministry of Transport. I'm to conduct an official enquiry as regards the future of this line. I understand I'm expected at the village hall. *(Taking Coggett's arm)* I trust it's within walking distance?

Edna (*tearing him away from Coggett*) It is indeed, sir. Allow me to accompany you there, sir.

Vernon Carry your bags, sir?

Ruddock I can manage, thank you all the same.

Vernon wrestles Ruddock's briefcase from him

Vernon No, no. I absolutely insist, sir.

Edna This way, sir...

They lead him off, competing for his attention

Coggett is left busily fixing her make-up

Vernon comes back to get her

Vernon Coggett!

Vernon exits and Coggett follows him off

Scene 8
The Village Hall

The audience of this play are the audience for the inquiry

Blakeworth enters, perhaps greeting a few individual members of the audience (ad lib). He eventually addresses the audience – perhaps beginning with a brief ad lib about something specific to the venue/ locality – before continuing

Blakeworth Thank you all for attending. It's good to see such a turn-out. I know many of you, as do I, consider this railway business a matter of great local concern. And indeed I uh — I fully expect Mr Ruddock from the Ministry of Transport to join us shortly. I, myself, unfortunately, won't be able to stay for the duration of the meeting. Pressing council business requires that I be elsewhere. One cannot under-estimate the importance of a few rounds of golf with the President of the Rotary Club. It's the oiling of such illustrious wheels that ensures the business life of this district runs smoothly.

Ruddock, Vernon, Coggett and Edna enter

Ah, here we are. (*To Ruddock*) Mr Ruddock, I presume. Blakeworth, town clerk, at your service, sir. If you could put me at the top of your agenda, sir. As I do have to get off to——

Ruddock Quiet please, everybody! Thank you. Let's keep this as brief as possible. Now it seems to me the matter in hand is straightforward enough. We all know why we're here. And the outcome of this enquiry all boils down to a question of safety first. Now, from my extensive research hereabouts——

Vernon, Coggett, Edna and Blakeworth join the audience – Edna and Vernon on separate sides. Ad lib comments with the audience and each other where relevant

Edna He's only just this minute got off the bloomin' train!

Ruddock —You'll speak when you're called to so do, madam, if you don't mind. There are proper procedures to be followed. Now, as I was saying, there's no doubting the fact that Titfield people as a whole are somewhat disturbed at the idea of an amateur-run railway.

Vernon Hear, hear.

Ruddock Now, no doubt, many of those opposed have reasons of their own for feeling as they do. Perhaps that will become clearer as the meeting proceeds. I call upon Mr Vernon Crump.

Vernon Here, sir.

Edna This'll be good.

Ruddock Speak up then, man.

Vernon has gone to the trouble of having someone write his speech down, so he delivers it very badly, and is made more uncomfortable by Edna's interjections

Edna Nice piece of paper, Crump. Get it the right way up, there's a good chap.

Vernon (*failing to note punctuation*) "I feel Mr Ruddock" ——

Edna (*laughing*) Oh dear. Priceless. "I feel Mr Ruddock"!

Vernon (*reading with care*) —"I feel, Mr Ruddock, sir, that there are very grave dangers involved in allowing a group of untrained amateurs to set up and operate a privately-owned railway. And having said the above" ——

Edna The above! The man's clearly a buffoon——

Vernon —"I feel the only adequate solution to the current predi — ca"——

Edna
Coggett } (*together*) Predicament!

Vernon —"predicament would be to have a local transport operative run an efficient omnibus service to replace the discontinued train service. Forthwith."

Ruddock And what is your interest in these proceedings, Mr Crump?

Vernon I am the proprietor of Crump and Son Road Transport Company, sir.

Edna And he's the nerve to call us amateurs.

Ruddock Well, Crump, this is all very interesting I'm sure, but you're hardly an unbiased voice in this matter, are you? I do so wish I could be sure of at least one impartial view.

Ruddock anxiously encourages Coggett to take the floor, but Blakeworth rises, much to the disgust of the others – who consider him a bore. They groan and grumble accordingly

Blakeworth I think I am able to provide that, sir. As town clerk I'm witness firsthand to the ebb and flow of grassroots opinion hereabouts——

Edna The only grass he sees is that patch around the nineteenth hole.

Blakeworth —and I feel it my public duty to say that the main opposition does indeed arise from a genuine doubt as to whether the ladies and gentlemen concerned would be capable of providing a safe and efficient service. Should however, you decide they can——

Edna Might I be permitted to speak?

Blakeworth can sneak out at any point from now, and enter as Weech whenever convenient

Ruddock You are?

During the next speech, Vernon whispers to Coggett

Edna Edna Chesterford. I'm one of the "ladies and gentlemen concerned" that Mr Blakeworth referred to, and I'd just like to point out that all those involved in this enterprise have recently enrolled to undertake an intensive course of professional tuition in the relevant areas of railway operation.

When Coggett speaks she is supposed to be putting on a Welsh accent – but this is neither reliable or accurate

Coggett Where, how, and who from?

Vernon Good question, ma'am.

Ruddock And who might you be, my dear?

Coggett The name's Ellen Coggett. I'm here to lodge a protest on behalf of the National—— (*Struggling to remember*)

Vernon Association of Railway Workers.

Coggett —Association of Railway Workers.

Ruddock I see. And what exactly is the nature of your protest, Miss Coggett?

Coggett My association would take a grave——

Vernon Welsh. Welsh.

Coggett (*continuing with a more pronounced Welsh accent*) —would take a grave view of any proposals to employ non-union staff on this line in flagrant disregard of the scale of wages already laid down for genuinely affiliated railway workers.

Vernon Hear, hear!

Edna Hold on! You tell us where we can get some genuine railway workers, and we'll use them with pleasure — at full union rates.

Coggett My association is not an employment bureau. My association is concerned only to restrict divisive division of the labour market, and to prevent the general exploitation of cheap labour.

Hopefully Weech has had time to enter by this point

Edna But we're asking to be exploited!

Weech And we're united in that!

Ruddock Pardon me, and who might you be sir?

Weech Sam Weech. I'll be driving the train.

Vernon Heaven help us all.

Weech (*to Edna*) Who's that woman?

Edna Association of Railway Workers.

Weech Really? She does look strangely familiar.

Ruddock If we could get on, gentlemen...and lady. You were saying, Miss Coggett.

Coggett With all due respect to your reverence, it doesn't matter what you want. It's simply my association's absolute duty to ensure that workers are not exploited by bosses. I fear I can put my case no clearer.

Weech But we are the bosses!

Edna Exactly. And in our company there's no quarrel at all between capital and labour.

Coggett My association will view any such situation as evidence of exploitation. And will take drastic steps to ensure that such exploitation does not continue. (*Flirting with Ruddock*) That's my final word on the matter. Now if you'll excuse me I have pay negotiations to conclude elsewhere.

Coggett gestures to Vernon that this means he should pay her

Ruddock Thank you very much, Miss Coggett.

Vernon attempts to pass an envelope of money to Coggett without anyone noticing

Coggett I did my best, Mr Crump. Though I must say I am used to more glamorous roles.
Weech I knew it. She's no workers representative. That's Tallulah Broadstairs, the music hall artiste. I'd know her anywhere. The Amazonian Harlot. (*Beat*) It's an act she does.
Edna Best keep the lid on that one I think, Sam?
Weech What? Oh, quite so, quite so.
Edna But it just proves that Crump's prepared to go to any lengths.
Weech At least we know what we're up against.
Ruddock If I could call this meeting to order, once again, Mr Weech. This is supposed to be a public enquiry, not the vicarage tea party. To conclude: as an old railway man myself, I cannot help sympathizing with those people who want to keep this line in operation. And it is apparent that they are determined to make every effort to adequately fit themselves for their duties. However...in their undoubted enthusiasm, I don't think they realize quite as clearly as the rest of the community what an enormous responsibility such an undertaking would be. In view of this, I do not feel justified in recommending that they should be granted the right to permanently take over the running of the Titfield to Mallingford line——
Edna You realize you're condemning our village to death? Open it up to buses and lorries, and what's it going to be like in five years time? Our houses will have numbers instead of names, there'll be traffic lights and zebra crossings and goodness knows what highway paraphenalia. With the result that it'll be twice as dangerous. It's the beginning of the end, this. And there's no romance in bus travel you know. (*Pointedly towards Vernon*) Great lumbering smelly things!
Vernon It's safer by bus. It's a much-quoted fact, that.
Edna Much quoted by you. (*To Ruddock*) We're not even asking for a monopoly as they are. All we're asking for is the chance to keep a valuable and much-loved service running.
Vernon Much-loved by who? A couple of twits who want to play at trains.
Edna Mr Ruddock, Mr Blakeworth spoke frankly earlier about how some people were scared of the implications of our desires. But if you'd just give us the opportunity we're asking for, we can prove that we can run this service safely and efficiently. People often don't realize what they have till it's gone. Don't let that happen here, sir.

Don't condemn us to a future of regrets. Just grant us this one small chance, sir. Because it means everything to our village. We want this railway. And we want to run it!

Applause

Weech Well said, Edna. Hear, hear.
Ruddock Thank you for being so forthright...and indeed so eloquent, madam. Now if you'll allow me to finish. I was about to add that although I do not feel justified in recommending that any permanent order be made, I do believe that you deserve the chance of proving your capabilities. I therefore intend to recommend to my minister that you be granted a probationary period of one month, as from Monday the sixteenth of June, nineteen fifty-two, after which, an inspector of Railways, appointed by the minister, shall report - detailing whether or not the efficiency with which the line is run justifies the said order being made permanent. And may I say — the Best of British!

Edna
Weech } (*together*) Hooray. Thank you sir, thank you sir.

Applause

Vernon One month! You won't last five minutes.
Ruddock Now, I must make my way back to Mallingford, there to catch my London connection.
Edna Will you take the train, sir?
Ruddock Thank you, no. In the interests of impartiality I think it only correct I sample the delights of Mr Crump's omnibus service.
Weech May the Lord go with you.
Vernon We don't need the Lord on board, Mr Weech. It's a well-known fact ——

Edna
Weech
Vernon } (*together*) It's safer by bus!

Taped music, if necessary, to bridge scenes

SCENE 9
Titfield Railway Station / On The Train / On The Bus

The station calendar now tells us it's Monday 16th June, 1952

Joan enters and addresses one side of the audience – who are now the passengers on the train. Dan is now in the audience

Joan Make yourselves comfortable ladies and gentlemen. We'll be leaving soon. And I'd like to take this opportunity to thank you for travelling on the Titfield-Mallingford Express.

Vernon enters

Vernon Titfield Titanic'd be a better name for her in my opinion.
Joan We guarantee you a safe and pleasant journey.
Vernon (*addressing the other side of the audience, who are seated on his bus*) Welcome to Crump and Son's Mallingford Flyer. I hope you're sitting comfortably. Why put your lives in the hands of amateurs? It's safer by bus. (*Approaching an audience member on the train side*) My carriage awaits if you'd care to reconsider, Madam. You look a little nervous. Are you sure you'd not rather travel with Crump and Son? We attract a better class of customer, as you can see. Now have you all got your tickets?

Weech and Edna enter in their railway uniforms

Weech You've done a grand job with these outfits, Joanie, at such short notice.
Vernon You look like a couple of over-dressed ice-cream salesmen.
Joan I did my best, Uncle.
Edna We appreciate it, Joan, everything you've done.
Joan It's not just me, Uncle, nearly the whole village has rallied round, helping make sure we're ready on time.
Vernon Don't know why you're all looking at me. You've as much chance of running this line successfully as a man has of walking on the moon.
Weech You are without faith, Mr Crump, and that distresses me. A more regular attendance at St Mary's would do you no harm.
Vernon I were there to marry and bury my wife, Mr Weech. And I'll be back to marry my son, and bury myself. That's enough religification for any man in my opinion.
Edna "Marry your son"! You're assuming that a creature might be found prepared to give young Harry house-room, Mr Crump.
Joan (*flustered*) Well, time we were off.
Weech Many aboard, Joan?
Joan It's nearly full, Uncle. I think it's going to prove a very popular service.
Edna Where's Dan? He's supposed to be up front with you, Sam.
Joan He went to help set up the bar. I don't think Mr Valentine had realized that he was to serve the customers in addition to helping himself.

Edna I'd better go and see if they're ready.

Weech Leave it, Edna. Clifton is a more than capable relief fireman. We'll manage perfectly without Dan. Besides, I must confess much of his advice is still ringing in my ears, so forthrightly was it offered. (*He goes to take up his position in the engine*)

Mrs Bottomley enters wielding a formidable handbag

Edna Oh, here's a straggler.

Vernon Crump and Son at your service, Mrs Bottomley, ma'am. Room for a small one at the back. Let me help you with your bag.

Mrs Bottomley Hey, hey, get off me. I want to travel in style!

Joan Hurry up there, Mrs Bottomley, the Titfield Express is just about to leave.

Vernon It's safer by bus, Mrs Bottomley.

Edna Nonsense, Crump. Let the train take the strain, Mrs Bottomley. I say, Joan, that's rather good, don't you think?

Vernon Big girls blouse.

Mrs Bottomley Very poetic, Mr Chesterford. Is there a bar on board, Miss?

Joan Last carriage, Mrs Bottomley.

Edna You'll find Mr Valentine presiding.

Vernon He'll be bladdered before you reach Fincham Junction.

Mrs Bottomley Jolly good.

Mrs Bottomley bumbles on and exits

Vernon Ah, she'll regret it, and serve her right. Fred Karno's bloomin army. If you make it all the way to Mallingford, Lady C, I'll eat my socks.

Edna *Bon appétite*, Crump, *bon appétite*.

Edna goes towards the back of the train

Joan The train about to leave is the eight-forty-seven service to Mallingford Town! The eight-forty-seven service to Mallingford Town is now leaving!

Weech eases the train out of the station. Meanwhile, Vernon sits down in the driver's seat of the bus and — cursing — struggles to start the knackered old thing

Vernon C'mon, Winston, crank the flamin' handle!

Vernon eventually pulls off in the direction of Mallingford

And we're away! Ladies and gentlemen, Mallingford or bust!

Joan walks down the train

Joan Tickets, please. Tickets from Titfield. *(If possible, tickets might have already been issued to members of the audience)*
Vernon (*to an unseen pedestrian*) Morning, Neville!
Joan (*to members of the audience*) Thank you, sir. Change at Mallingford for Nottingham. Platform one. Thank you, madam. Change at Fincham for Leeds. Platform three. (*To an audience member who is obviously with her partner*) I see you've brought your father along, madam. Well, it's a day out for him, isn't it?

Edna comes forward from the back of the train

Edna Everything all right, Joan?
Joan Fine thanks, Lady Chesterford.
Vernon Watch out! Cattle grid. (*He judders up and down as he speeds across it*)
Joan Everything seems to be proceeding very smoothly, Lady Chesterford.
Edna No thanks to old Dan. Where on earth's he got to? Not that his absence appears to be a problem. You know I've a feeling Sam was born to the task.
Joan It's given him a new lease of life, you asking him to help run the railway. (*To a member of the audience*) Lavatory's that way, sonny, if you need to go. But don't be running in the corridor!
Vernon We're catching them up!
Edna Isn't this exciting, Joan? Look at that view. I'd find it breathtaking even if it wasn't part of my estate. The countryside must be preserved, Joan, at all cost, for the enjoyment and benefit of everyone. Except poachers and ramblers, of course. I say – look – there's Crump and his ghastly omnibus!
Joan They're gaining on us!
Vernon Hump-back bridge! (*He comes up off his seat as he races across it*)
Edna Tunnel coming up.

The Lights go out on the train and the train whistle sounds. When the Lights come back on Edna races to the other side of the train. As the bus would now be on the other side of the train

Edna
Joan } (*together*) There they are!

Edna makes gestures at the bus, then remembering the passengers, is embarrassed

Edna Is it hot in here or is it just me? I can open a window if you'd like ma'am. Or is that your natural complexion? (*She walks up the train acknowledging the passengers*) Morning. Morning. Morning. (*One of them is Dan*) Morning, Dan. (*Dragging him out*) Dan, where the devil did you get to?

Dan I were helping Mr Valentine with the bar, Lady C. He's having difficulty orientating himself, being so used to standing on the other side like.

Joan But he is managing all right now?

Dan Oh aye. He's happy as a pig in muck. Pardon me, Miss Weech. Left him up there singing *All Things Bright and Beautiful* and dancing a tango with Mrs Bottomley.

Edna I say. Is it really possible to tango to hymns, Joan?

Joan I'm sure I wouldn't know, Lady Chesterford.

Edna Ah well. So long as he remembers to serve the customers. But shouldn't you be up front with Mr Weech, Dan, watching over him with your expert eye?

Dan He don't need my expert eye nor no-one else's. I may not have much time for his church speechifying, Miss Weech, but I'll say this for him, your uncle do know how to drive a train.

Joan He'd be very proud to hear you say that, Mr Taylor, I'm sure.

Dan (*looking out of window*) Ah, well that's as maybe, but this here's where I get off.

Dan jumps off and runs on the spot whilst moving backwards – to give the impression that the train is leaving him behind

Edna What are you doing, man? You can't alight from the train while she's moving.

Dan I'll catch you up at Ravens Wood!

Edna Well I'll be — I don't believe it. He intends to poach on my land! Dan! Dan? You old rascal.

Joan Surely the odd rabbit can't hurt, Lady Chesterford. And Mr Taylor has been very useful to you of late. He seems to be able to turn his hand to anything, does our Dan.

Edna That's what worries me. I say! What's happening now?

Joan We appear to be slowing down.

Edna I thought it was all too good to last.

They are rocked slightly by the motion of the train slowing

Joan Don't panic, ladies and gentlemen, I'm sure we'll be resuming our journey shortly.

Meanwhile, tootling along in the bus, Vernon suddenly seems to have cheered up considerably. He laughs to himself

Vernon Ha ha! I've gotta have a look at this. We'll be taking an unscheduled stop 'ere, ladies and gentlemen, to witness the perils of free enterprise. Smoke 'em if you got 'em. Ha ha! Oh, this'll be good!

The train has stopped. Weech is distressed

Edna What's going on, Sam?
Weech There's something on the line, Edna.
Edna What d'you mean "something"? A cow? An avalanche? A leaf? Speak up, man.
Weech A steamroller.
Joan Harry Crump, I'll murder you!
Weech I fear you'll have to find him first, Joan. He's nowhere to be seen. I'm afraid we're well and truly stuck.
Joan Oh, he won't have gone far. No doubt he's skulking under a nearby stone, and peeping out to enjoy the fun. (*Marching off purposefully*) It won't take me a minute to unearth him. I shall just have to follow my nose.

Joan exits

Vernon Trouble, Lady C? That's the trouble with railway track, see. Needs to be maintained, or all sorts of accidents are liable to occur. No doubt professionals'd know about these things...
Edna And no doubt you're behind this in some way, Mr Crump?
Weech I must say, I had thought young Harry above this kind of prank. And I don't think I was alone in having had certain hopes for the lad.
Edna They do say an apple never falls far from the tree. Like father, like son, eh Crump?
Vernon There'll be deeper forces working away, 'neath that boy's savage breast.
Edna You've lost me completely now, I'm afraid.

Vernon Yes well, you were never one to put affairs of the heart before concerns of the purse, were you, Lady Chesterford?
Edna I must say that's pretty rich coming from you. You made poor Mrs Crump's life a living hell.
Vernon Ah, but that were a mutual arrangement, blessed by the church, no less.
Weech Yes, and this all very well, but it's not going to help us reach Mallingford, Edna. Which is what these good people have paid us to do.

Joan comes on, leading Harry by the ear

Edna Ah. So is this your doing, Harry Crump?
Harry I'm sure I don't know what you mean, ma'am.
Joan That hulking great contraption blocking the line is yours, Harry, is it not?
Edna Yes, come on. What's the meaning of this, Harry?
Harry She just broke down on me, Lady Chesterford. Temperamental shrew that she is. (*To Joan*) I'm talking about the steamroller now, miss. (*To Edna*) When she gets like this she'll respond to neither kind words nor brute reason. I wish I could help you, but there it is, it's out of my hands.
Joan You won't even attempt to move it?
Harry Oh I've tried, Miss Weech, but like I say, there are some so wilful as never could be moved.
Vernon What we talking about now then, Harry?
Joan The steamroller, Mr Crump! Which happens to be the sole topic of conversation here!
Vernon Begging your pardon, miss!
Weech Now look here, Harry...
Joan Leave this to me, please, Uncle.
Weech Yes, dear.
Edna Now see here, Crump, you young scallywag ——
Joan Lady Chesterford. Please don't interrupt.
Edna Ah — right.
Joan So you're saying, Harry Crump, that you intend to leave that lump of useless metal in our path. And you are determined moreover, that you will not consider any further attempts to remove it.
Harry In not quite as many words, aye.
Joan Not even for me, Mr Crump?
Harry For you, Miss Weech?
Joan Yes, Harry. For me. (*With considerable effort*) Pretty please.
Harry Well now, were such sweet words to be accompanied by a

kiss...

Joan That's it! I'm sorry, Harry, I'm not in the mood to play your games. Uncle, is this locomotive strong enough to force Mr Crump's infernal machine from the track?

Weech Well, I don't know my dear, Dan's the person I'd ordinarily ask. Any idea where he's got to?

They realize Dan can't possibly be there

Edna Off poaching on my land, no doubt.

Joan Then we're just going to have to try to make a decision without him.

Weech Ah. Well we might be able to shunt the steamroller from the track without incurring too much damage to ourselves.

Vernon If you had half the sense you were born with you'd know when to give up on a bad job.

Joan I don't recall anybody asking you for your advice, Mr Crump.

Edna We certainly need to do something, Sam, and quickly, if we're ever to make up the time we've lost.

Weech I suppose we could always give it a try.

Joan Fine. Then it's decided. (*To the passengers*) We won't be keeping you much longer, ladies and gentlemen, we're just about to dispose of a very minor irritation. (*Shouting*) Crank her up to full power, Uncle, or whatever it is you do. Then full steam ahead at the enemy's bows!

Harry Wait a minute, you can't do that!

Joan I think you'll find, Mr Crump, that a determined woman can do most anything she sets her mind to... (*Shouting*) Forward men!

Harry All right, I'll move her!

Joan (*as she exits*) Full steam ahead!

Joan exits

Harry (*to the audience*) God I love that woman.

Horrendous scraping, metallic, destructive noise as the train gradually nudges the steamroller aside. (Noise can be made by cast, utilising whatever is to hand – or be pre-recorded)

Harry, afeared for his steamroller, runs off

Edna Thar she blows! Looks like it's cheese on toast for you tonight, Crump!

Joan looks aghast

What's up, Joan?

Joan I've a feeling I've just made the biggest mistake of my life.

Edna Nonsense, Joan, you were well within your rights.

Joan I'm never really sure what's best, to be ruled by one's heart, or one's head.

Edna I'll confess, Joan, I'm not *au fait* with such considerations. All I know is, we're back on course and that's as should be. So stiff upper lip and reassure the passengers, there's a good chap.

Harry enters holding a huge chain

Harry She's a right mess, Dad. They've severed the drive chain.

Vernon Oh aye? Well I'd better be pressing on, if I'm ever gonna get this lot to Mallingford.

Harry But it'll take me ages to get her back in working order. And my estimate for the Ravens Wood contract went in today. I could be starting in a few weeks.

Vernon We'll have a look at her later, son. Whatever happens, they're gonna regret what they've done to you. I'll see to that, boy. If it's the last thing I do.

Joan Ladies and gentlemen, might I take this opportunity to apologize for our recent delay. Please rest assured that things are now back to normal and we are pleased to again be offering a full service. In fact, if you'd all like to retire to the bar for fifteen minutes, you'll find an extensive range of drinks and light refreshments on offer. Once again, we thank you for travelling with Titfield Railways, and we hope you'll rejoin us for the rest of our journey.

Train noise to fade

CURTAIN

ACT II

SCENE 1
In The Countryside

This scene can take place anywhere in the auditorium – amongst the audience – or in the aisles – or on the darkened stage

It is night-time and dark

Harry and Vernon enter, with torches. Vernon is carrying a shotgun

Owls hoot etc., scaring them. (Offstage cast members can voice any night-creatures)

Harry Dad...?
Vernon What?
Harry What are we doing here?
Vernon Shh. (*Low*) All my life I've missed whatever targets I've set for myself. Well, tonight, that's gonna change. I won't be wide of the mark this time.
Harry (*low*) But what are we supposed to be hunting? There's no game in these parts.
Vernon The game, Harry, is making sure the general public can travel safely and efficiently in the future. By bus. (*He spies his target, which is out of sight of the audience*) There she is. Once we've made certain that thing won't hold water, those idiots plans'll go the same way.
Harry You're going to shoot the water tower?
Vernon A master-stroke, eh?
Harry But what about the train?

Vernon laughs

I'm not sure about this, Dad.
Vernon The quicker it's done, son, the quicker we can get back and start trying to rebuild that steamroller of yours.
Harry Hold on, Dad, where'd you get your hands on a gun in the first place?
Vernon I happened across it, Harry, purely by chance.

Harry Where?
Vernon In Lady C's gun cabinet. Now can we stop nattering and get down to the business in hand?

He fires the gun. Water splashes down on Harry

Harry Dad?

Vernon laughs. They exit

SCENE 2
On The Train

Joan walks forward from the back of the auditorium

Edna comes down the other side

Lights come up on the audience – the train passengers now constitute the entire audience

Edna I must say, Joan, I can't believe how well things have taken off. It's incredible. Seems we've twice as many passengers as when we first started running the line.
Joan It's true, Lady Chesterford, ticket sales are up one hundred percent. But unfortunately that has caused a slight problem.
Edna A problem, Joan?
Joan They appear to be a thirsty lot. Mr Valentine says the bar's in danger of running dry. We've one bottle of gin left but once that's gone...
Edna I did notice there was a pretty uncivilized dash to the bar earlier.
Joan They'll all just have to cut back on their intake.
Edna (*to an audience member*) I'm sure that won't be easy for you, Mrs Compton-Chamberlain, I know you like your gin.
Joan Tunnel coming up.

The auditorium is plunged into complete darkness. There are whistles and other noise as they go through the tunnel

Lights up suddenly to reveal Dan pressed up against the outside of the train window, clinging on for dear life and carrying a sack. (*It doesn't matter if there isn't an actual window, the actor can simply mime his predicament*)

Edna opens the window to help Dan through. (*Loud train noise when window is opened*)

They try to talk but the train noise is too loud with the window still open

Edna mimes shutting the window. Now they can hear themselves speak

Dan Morning, Lady C. Miss Weech.
Edna Dan, nice of you to join us. Been out poaching on my land again, no doubt.
Dan I wouldn't say poaching, Lady C, no.
Edna Would you not. Then what's in the bag, pray tell?
Dan That's a hare, me lady, I can't tell a lie. Thing is, me lady, they're vermin, see. If you don't keep the population under control, it upsets the balance of nature. And they breed like rabbits, you know. Beg pardon, Miss Weech.
Edna So you're saying that you're actually doing me a favour, Dan?
Dan You could say that, yes, ma'am.
Edna And what about pheasant? Are they vermin, too?
Dan They — are ma'am, yes. They do need keeping down.
Edna Well do your best, then, Dan. Your help will be much appreciated. Come to think of it, I've a gun at the Manor you could borrow if it'd be of any use. D'you know, I may have misjudged you, Dan...
Dan No offence taken, ma'am.
Edna Ah, what's this? We seem to have stopped.

Joan checks her watch

Joan Nothing to be concerned about, ladies and gentlemen, we've simply stopped to fill up with water. We'll be on our way again shortly.

Weech comes down from his engine

What is it, Uncle, you look as white as a sheet?
Weech We've a problem, Dan.
Edna What is it?
Weech Some idiot's peppered the water crane with buckshot. It's useless.
Edna Vernon Crump, no doubt. That scoundrel's become the bane of my life. If I ever get hold of him I'll——
Weech That won't solve our immediate dilemma, Edna.

Valentine enters

Valentine What's going on? Somebody thrown a party and not invited me?

Edna Sabotage, Mr Valentine.

Valentine I say. How dashed exciting.

Weech We're in danger of running out of water.

Valentine Never touch the stuff, so that'll not affect me. Ah. I see. Train needs it right? Quite. Hot water we're in then, or not. What? I'll shut up, shall I? Yes? For the best.

Joan The question is: can we make it from here to Mallingford on what we've got?

Edna Dan?

Dan It's unlikely.

Edna But we're desperate, Dan!

Dan Well — not unless we drop the fire, ma'am.

Weech Drop the fire! And lose my honour as a driver? Never!

Dan Then she'll blow up.

They give a collective gasp

Joan What if we top up what we've got? Will that at least get us there?

Weech But that's the problem, Joan.

Edna What are you thinking of, Joan?

Dan The bar.

Valentine I say...

Edna But you just said we——

Joan We're nearly out of alcohol. But we've got the water for washing up.

Valentine Quite right. In fact, I must confess, haven't got round to doing any of that yet.

Dan Then it might just be enough. If we're careful.

Edna But how are we going to get it to the front of the train?

Joan Containers. Anything we can lay our hands on. Mr Valentine, I suggest you go and make a start. Pass the receptacles forward down the train the minute they're filled.

Valentine rushes to the back of the train – which is at the back of the audience

Uncle, go and prepare to take water on board. We're far from beaten yet. (*To the audience*) We're going to need your help here, ladies and gentlemen. So if you're given a receptacle, please pass it forward.

Edna Yes, don't just sit there gawping – the sooner she's topped up, the sooner we can be on our way.

Joan (*to audience*) Come on, ladies and gentlemen, lend a hand!

Edna (*to an audience member*) Cheer up sir, it's not the end of the world. You can't be that anxious to get to Mallingford. Oh I see, you've tickets for the music hall. Tallulah Broadstairs, eh? Mum's the word.

Containers begin to be passed forward from the back. Perhaps 'busy' instrumental music plays low under this. Devise lines during rehearsal that relate to the containers used. Containers can range from sensible everyday receptacles to bizarre items from Lost Property. Possible containers can be: a fire bucket, an army helmet, Valentine's tankard, an ice bucket, an empty gin bottle, a saucepan, a tea-pot, a vase (that someone is taking back to the shop for a refund – gag about taste), a bed pan or a potty, Mrs Bottomley's handbag, a beer barrel (include a joke about the water content of local beer), Mr Blakeworth's hat, etc. Anything that might be part of the construction of the train later can obviously be put to use now – so that it will be handy when it's needed

Is that enough, Sam?
Weech A teeny drop more?
Valentine There's no more water. But...

Valentine gallantly surrenders his hip flask. Silence as he bravely witnesses the loss of its contents

Weech That's made the difference!
Dan She's as ready as she'll ever be.
Edna Excellent, Dan. We'll be off any minute now, ladies and gentlemen.
Joan Thank you for your patience, and your assistance.
Edna Mr Valentine, as soon as we get back to Titfield I shall buy you a drink at *The Pig and Whistle*.

The cast make the noise of the train as she speeds up and moves off. The train noises continue as the lights fade and the cast disperse to swiftly assemble again at...

Scene 3
The Pig and Whistle Public House

Valentine, Weech, Edna enter, excitedly talking together

Joan (*off*) Fine then, Fred, you get off, I'll lock up again tonight.

Joan enters
Last orders, please, ladies and gentlemen.

Edna Last orders, Joan? On a day such as this?

Joan Laws are laws, Lady C.

Valentine Besides, d'you know, funny thing, I think I've had sufficient.

Joan But you always order another treble at last orders, Mr Valentine.

Valentine I'm a changed man, Joan. D'you know, I never imagined I'd hold down a position of responsibility again. But the thrill this business has given me knocks the booze into a cocked hat, I don't mind telling you.

Weech It really has been quite an extraordinary day. I don't think I've ever been as happy in my entire life.

Edna We're a cracking team, it has to be said.

Joan That's time at the bar then, ladies and gentlemen.

Valentine Well here's to us!

Harry slips in unnoticed

Edna And to an even more successful future!

Weech What we need to concentrate on now – is the inspector's visit tomorrow.

Edna We'll sail through.

Valentine We've more than proved capable.

Edna Despite the best efforts of Mr Crump.

Joan spots Harry

Joan I've just called time, I'm afraid, Harry.

Harry It weren't a drink I was wanting, but a word with Lady Chesterford. About the railway.

Edna Well speak up, lad.

Valentine You have the floor, sir!

Harry I was hoping — in private like.

Edna The railway, as you well know, Harry, concerns all of those present.

Harry Well — it's Dad, really.

Valentine Ah.

Edna His name's something of a dirty word around here, I'm afraid, Harry.

Harry He knows that. And that's why he asked me to come and see you. It's just that — well, he's very impressed with what you've achieved, like.

Valentine As well he might be.

Harry And he's sure that this railway inspector'll be impressed too.

Edna It's odds on.

Harry But that doesn't necessarily mean he'll grant a permanent licence, does it?
Weech What's your point, Harry?
Harry Well Dad feels, that if this railway inspector were to learn that there were no longer any alternative form of transport here in Titfield, then he'd grant you your licence like a shot.
Edna Hold on. No more buses, you mean?
Valentine So Crump's finally throwing in the towel. Splendid news.
Harry Not exactly throwing in the towel, no.
Weech Then what?
Harry Dad says he'd be prepared to consider a merger. If you let him come in with you, fifty-fifty, he'll drop all opposition forthwith.
Valentine Blighter's gone bust has he?
Joan I think you'll find that's a libellous statement, Mr Valentine.
Valentine It is? I do apologize. I'd really no idea.
Harry Anyway. I've said what I came to say. That's his offer. Take it or leave it.
Valentine The idea's preposterous!
Weech You're a nice lad, Harry, and I for one am sorry for any rifts this business has caused...
Edna But the fact remains, Harry, that sooner than agree to a partnership with your father, I'd see our train reduced to scrap, or dumped in the river. And I imagine I speak for all of us when I say that?
Valentine Quite right.
Edna I'm sorry, old chap. Now, as your plea appears to have put a damper on proceedings, I think I'll turn in. Busy day tomorrow.
Valentine A mere formality, Edna. I'll walk along with you, if you don't mind.
Edna See you outside, Sam?

Valentine and Edna exit

Weech Umm — yes. (*Concerned*) You'll not be long, Joan?
Joan I'll be along presently, Uncle. And I'll be fine, honestly.

Weech exits

There's an awkward silence between Joan and Harry

Joan How's your steamroller now?
Harry Fine. Dad helped me fix it.
Joan That was kind.
Harry Yes. (*He pauses*) I've got the contract to clear the path through

Ravens Wood. Start tomorrow.

Joan Well done.

Harry Well, it was touch and go. After...you know.

Joan I'm sorry, Harry, I really am. I just…don't know what came over me, really. I won't ask that you forgive me. I'm sure things have...gone too far for that.

Harry You make a formidable opponent, Joan.

Joan Is that your way of calling me a right old dragon?

Harry No! No...

Joan Well, what's done is done. I must get on. I am glad you put everything right in time to get that contract, Harry. You must have worked hard. You deserve to do well. I'm sorry things — ended up like this. (*Busying herself*) But there we are – no sense crying over spilt milk. No doubt one day you'll meet somebody and — well, she'll be very proud of you, I'm sure. Now I'm afraid I must ask you to leave. As I'm always telling Mr Valentine, the law's the law.

Joan starts to usher him out, but he turns back to her

Harry Joan?

Joan Harry?

Harry I hope — I hope there are others like you.

Joan I don't think that's very likely, Harry, do you?

SCENE 4
Near The Engine Shed

It is night-time and dark. Off stage the cast make night noises

Vernon is onstage using a pick-axe to pull up railway line

Blakeworth enters with a torch. He is wearing his coat over his pyjamas and has a night-cap protruding from beneath his bowler hat

Vernon hides

Blakeworth Hallo? Is anybody there? I thought I heard somebody go by. If — if you're in distress I might be able to assist. And if you're up to no good then I must warn you that I've instructed my wife to contact the police if I don't return in ten minutes. And if it's neither of the above please give details on a separate sheet of paper. Hallo? (*To himself*) Must be bloomin' imagining things. Best check further up the line.

Blakeworth bumbles off

Harry enters with a torch

Harry Dad?
Vernon (*picking him out with his own torch beam*) Harry. You took your time. All set?
Harry Yes. I think I might have woken Mr Blakeworth when I drove past his house.
Vernon You did. Bloomin typical, he spends all day every day asleep at his desk – then stays awake all night sticking his beak in where it's not wanted.
Harry Dad?
Vernon What now?
Harry I don't think this is a good idea.
Vernon "I don't think this is a good idea." They'll put that on your flippin' headstone.
Harry But don't you see? It's not right, what we're doing.
Vernon And smashing up your steamroller was, was it? All I've done is made a few minor alterations to the track, that should be enough to re-route the train. It just remains to nudge her on her way.
Harry It seems such a waste, Dad.
Vernon You're too squeamish, Harry, that's your trouble. Besides, no-one's gonna get hurt. It's near enough the perfect crime. (*He plays his torch beam over the audience*) If there was only somebody to stick in the frame we'd be laughing. Come on, let's get on with it. Let's see how the Titfield Express runs after a proper dunking!

They both exit

Blakeworth comes back on, still nosing about. He watches the shenanigans going on off stage, open-mouthed. Many noises off through this

Vernon (*off*) Come on, let's get on with it. Up in the steamroller and start her up.
Harry (*off*) OK. Here we go then Dad.
Vernon (*off*) Bring her up to the engine.
Harry (*off*) Right Dad.
Vernon (*off*) To the left.
Harry (*off*) Left?
Vernon (*off*) Right.
Harry (*off*) Right?

Vernon (*off*) No, left! Ease her forward son, give her a shunt.

Noise off

She's moving son.
Blakeworth What d'you think you're doing?
Vernon (*off*) Faster!
Harry (*off*) She won't take much more of this, Dad!
Vernon (*off*) Push!
Harry (*off*) Can I ease her off now Dad?
Vernon (*off*) No!
Harry (*off*) Dad...?
Vernon (*off*) Brake!
Blakeworth Careful!
Vernon (*off*) There she goes!
Blakeworth The train's heading straight for the river!

We hear the train crash into the river. Water splashes Blakeworth and the audience. Blakeworth sets off to raise the alarm but runs straight into the torch-beam of Sergeant Wilson

Wilson Evening, sir.
Blakeworth You've got to do something!
Wilson I think you're right sir. It's a good job I happened by. Are those night-clothes you're wearing, sir?
Blakeworth That doesn't matter now! They've destroyed the Titfield Express!
Wilson I'd prefer if you'd let me decide what's relevant to this inquiry, sir. Do you make a habit of hanging about after dark improperly dressed?
Blakeworth I'm the Town Clerk for heavens sake.
Wilson Mitigating circumstances, eh sir? Pressure of the job getting to you, no doubt. Just my little joke, that, sir. Now if you'd be so kind as to come along with me, we'll have this little matter cleared up in next to no time. (*As he leads Blakeworth off*) If you'd furnish me with details of a sympathetic friend, sir.
Blakeworth My wife, sergeant.
Wilson You're married, sir? No doubt the wife doesn't understand you, eh? We're seeing more and more of this type of thing I'm afraid. Sign of the times, so they say.

SCENE 5
The Vicarage

Edna enters with Joan

Edna How is he?
Joan You can imagine. It's been a terrible blow.
Edna That goes for all of us, I'll warrant. If I'd have realized what lengths Crump was prepared to go to, I'd have treated his merger idea with a little more grace.
Joan You'd have considered a partnership with a man capable of such wilful destruction?
Edna I'd have remained happily ignorant of the excesses he was capable of – that's what I'm saying.
Joan It's easy to be wise after the event, Lady Chesterford. No matter what the consequences, I think you made the correct decision at the time.
Edna I'm not convinced, Joan. Never underestimate your enemy. He's achieved his victory it seems — in no uncertain terms — and left us floundering in no-man's land as a result.
Joan It does seem all is lost.
Edna The police are on their way, apparently. They seem to think they have a lead. Oh, by the way, I was looking out that old shotgun for Dan earlier this evening, and blow me down if it doesn't appear to be missing. Remind me to mention that to the police while they're here.
Joan Your shotgun, Lady Chesterford?
Edna Yes, Joan?
Joan The water tower, Lady Chesterford?
Edna (*finally catching on*) Good heavens, Joan! You don't think...? Well I never...

Weech enters

Joan Ah, Uncle. Lady Chesterford's here to see you.
Edna Sam?
Weech Edna. You face a man in spiritual crisis.
Edna Oh, Sam...
Weech I can't help feeling it's a judgement on me, d'you see?
Edna Nonsense, Sam. What more could you have done?
Weech I've failed in my duty. That such a crime could be committed in my parish.
Joan Is there no chance of salvage?
Edna It would take three months to mend her, even if we could raise her.

Weech And we have less than twenty-four hours.
Joan And there's no way they'd put off the inspection to allow us the time to get the repairs done?
Edna Red tape is strictly non-elastic. If there's no railway there tomorrow for the inspector to inspect, our order is automatically cancelled.
Weech In other words, we've had it.
Joan You must try to be brave, Uncle. Don't lose faith.

There is a ring at the door

Excuse me. (*She goes to answer the door*)
Edna It does appear that the writing's on the wall, Sam.
Weech If there's one thing I've learned since having Joan around, it's that it's always wise to respect her advice. Now if you don't mind, I think I shall pray, Edna.
Edna Good heavens.

Weech prays, facing the picture of "The Titfield Thunderbolt"

Meanwhile, to one side, Joan lets Sergeant Wilson in

Wilson Sergeant Wilson, miss.
Joan Joan Weech.
Wilson Are you all right, miss?
Joan Of course, sergeant, why do you ask?
Wilson You — appear to be staring at me, miss.
Joan I do? I'm sorry. You just — remind me of somebody else.
Wilson A handsome young fellow, I'll warrant. (*Beat*) Just my little joke, Miss.
Joan No—no, you're quite right. He is — most handsome. Very handsome indeed. (*She stares at him*)

Meanwhile Weech has been hit by a thunderbolt of an idea which Wilson and Joan approach and witness

Weech Eureka! Edna? Do you see what I see?
Edna Sam?

Weech grabs the picture from the wall

Weech The Titfield Thunderbolt! She's the answer to our prayers, Edna!

Perhaps he involuntarily grabs her hands here. A brief moment of pleasurable awkwardness

Wilson It is the Reverend Weech I've come to see, miss.
Edna But the Titfield Thunderbolt's been in Mallingford Museum for the past seventy-five years.
Weech She'll still take steam, Edna, I'm sure of it!
Joan Well, won't you come through, Sergeant?
Edna But how do we get her out of the museum and back into service?
Weech The town clerk. What's his name...?
Wilson Blakeworth?
Weech Blakeworth. He could authorize it at a moment's notice!
Wilson I'm afraid there may be a problem there, sir.
Weech Who's this?
Joan Sergeant Wilson, this is my uncle, the Reverend Sam Weech.
Wilson Pleased to meet you, sir. No relation to the infamous Weech of the counterfeit relic case, by any chance, sir?
Weech He's my brother, Sergeant. Joan's father.
Wilson Ah. Begging your pardon, miss.
Edna You said there was some problem regarding Mr Blakeworth?
Wilson We do have a Mr Blakeworth in custody, madam. I arrested him myself near the scene of the crime. He was— (*Trying to prevent Joan hearing*) —improperly attired, madam.
Weech You're not holding him in connection with the destruction of the Titfield Express?
Wilson That's correct, sir.
Edna I think, if you'll excuse me saying so, Sergeant, that you're barking up the wrong tree.
Weech Though Blakeworth was opposed to us running the line at the outset.
Edna But he's a local government officer, Sam - not a man of action.
Weech You must release Mr Blakeworth, Sergeant, forthwith – as we need him to assist us with a matter of extreme urgency.
Wilson Well I——
Joan And when you've done so, I suggest you proceed with haste to the home of a Mr Vernon Crump, for it is there you'll locate the weapon used for the destruction of the water tower near Fincham Junction.
Edna A weapon stolen from my premises earlier this week.
Weech So! To the police station, to release Blakeworth – and then to the Museum – to recommission The Titfield Thunderbolt! Hallelujah! All is not lost! (*He sees Wilson out*)

Sergeant Wilson exits

Edna Sam? Aren't you forgetting something? — The Titfield Thunderbolt only solves half the problem. It's an engine. We'll need a carriage if we're to run a passenger service.

They pause for thought

Weech
Joan (*together*) Dan!
Edna Dan?
Joan He lives in a railway carriage!
Edna But surely he'd never agree to...
Joan He might. If you were to put down in writing his hunting and fishing rights. Say — grant him a licence for the rest of his life.
Edna But it flies in the face of tradition, Joan!
Weech It is for the good of the community, Edna.
Edna By jove, you're right. In that case, I'll get over there right away. You'd best accompany me, Joan, old Dan's got a bit of a soft spot for you.
Weech I'll catch up with Sergeant Wilson then. There's much to do. The railway inspector's due in — twelve and a half hours.

Scene 6
Titfield Railway Station / On The Train

The station calendar is set at Monday 14th July, 1952

The carriage is transformed into Dan's carriage home, using an old, threadbare armchair, cushions, curtains, a standard lamp, a foot stool etc. Depending on budget the cast can also be constructing The Titfield Thunderbolt. (If it's a small budget then make The Titfield Thunderbolt here from found objects. If it's a budget which allows for a working life-size steam train to appear at the end of this scene then just furnish the carriage)

Dan, Weech and Joan are admiring the carriage, Edna is examining the coupling

Weech She's a beauty, isn't she Dan?
Dan She's been a comfortable enough home to me.
Weech I meant the Thunderbolt.
Dan Ah. I'd say we've done a grand job on both counts. If you'd asked

me twenty-four hours ago were it possible I'd have laughed in your face, Reverend.

Weech I seem to remember asking you twelve hours ago, Dan, and you doing just that.

Dan It were a triumph of faith, sir, no less. A triumph of faith.

Weech We've all good reason to be proud of the effort, Dan, you included.

Joan Of course, you'll have ridden the Thunderbolt before, perhaps, Mr Taylor? As a boy?

Dan Cheeky madam. I've seen her in the museum often enough, though.

Weech But to actually be — it's almost too good to believe.

Dan I did once ride the North Star. You know, Gooch's two-two-two, with the double crank driving axle and——

Weech I'm fully aware of what you speak, Dan. But even that surely pales into insignificance compared to this.

Edna comes up. She's in a bit of a fluster

Edna I've been looking at that coupling, Sam. I'm still not completely reassured.

Weech Well Dan's done the best he can. I think we should just go ahead and hitch her on.

Dan I'll take another look at her Lady C, if it'll make you feel better. But I think she'll suffice with a wing and a prayer.

Dan goes to do so

Weech He hasn't failed us yet, Edna.

Edna Who are you referring to, Sam, Dan, or the powers that be?

Weech Dan's doing his best. As for the Good Lord, well, today his mysterious ways will once again be put to the test.

Joan What's this about the coupling?

Edna The carriage and the engine don't marry. The coupling on the carriage didn't come in till thirty years later.

Weech Thirty-three to be precise. Eighteen seventy-five.

Joan But surely the inspector will never know the difference?

Weech It's not him that's the problem.

Edna If we have to use the brake in the van, it'd throw the weight of the whole train on to that coupling. And were that to happen...

Joan Good gracious. You're saying it wouldn't hold?

Edna It's possible that we might find ourselves separated from our means of locomotion, yes. In which case, it would take rather more than a prayer to get us all the way to Mallingford.

Weech But we must hope it won't come to that. It's too late now to do more than we have. I'll ring Mr Blakeworth, see if he can't put this inspector off for a few minutes more, while we connect her up.

Weech exits

Wilson and Vernon enter together

Wilson Ah, Lady Chesterford.

Joan Sergeant Wilson.

Wilson Miss.

Edna What the devil's going on?

Wilson I'm taking this fellow into custody, madam. He was apprehended whilst resisting arrest. We found your shotgun on his premises, just as you said. The suspect then took off in what could loosely be described as an omnibus, and drove in a reckless manner through Titfield and the surrounding by-ways. We gave chase in the Black Maria but during the course of that pursuit both vehicles sustained damage rendering them temporarily unroadworthy. Therefore I must insist that you permit us to board your train so that we can proceed forthwith to Mallingford Police Station.

Edna I'm afraid that's not possible, Sergeant.

Joan But Lady C——

Edna This is a private service, run solely for the purpose of enabling the railway inspector to make his assessment.

Wilson I fear you may have involuntarily misheard me, Lady Chesterford. I did in fact, employ the word insist in that last instruction.

Joan It looks as if we've no choice, Lady Chesterford.

Wilson Well put, miss.

Edna Oh, very well. There's a lock-up in the guards van.

Vernon and Wilson get on the train

Cornered at last then, Crump? And not before time.

Vernon I've got rights, you know. I want my Harry here. He should be with his dad in his hour of need.

Wilson (*aware that this could be difficult*) That's not possible, Mr Crump, and you know it.

Joan Surely Mr Crump's entitled to see his son, Sergeant Wilson?

Wilson Mr Crump Jr has been contacted, miss. But unfortunately he had to commence a very important job this morning in the Ravens Wood area.

Vernon He's deserted me, Miss Weech. Like a rat leaving a stinking ship.

Joan He must work, Mr Crump. You should be proud of the way that lad's stood on his own two feet.

Edna Quite so. Against all the odds young Harry appears to at last be making something of himself. And no thanks to you, Crump.

Vernon I knows I've done wrong. You don't need to tell me. And I do feel ashamed. Seems everybody's made a go of things round here but me. I mean, look at this train. It's a triumph, all right. That you've achieved all this in one night. It's enough to put a fellow back on the straight and narrow.

Wilson Move along there now, Crump. And don't even consider any funny business.

Vernon and Wilson start to exit

Vernon (*as they go*) Perhaps I can change, Miss Weech — mend me ways. For Harry's sake. You could do worse than him, you know.

Edna Sam. How's progress?

Weech A few minutes more.

Edna We don't have a few minutes.

Joan We're running late as it is.

Edna I presume you managed to stall the inspector.

Weech Mr Blakeworth has been entertaining Mr Clegg at the golf club. He said he'd try to persuade him to partake of another pot of tea, but he didn't sound hopeful.

Joan Did he give any idea of what we were to expect?

Edna Good thinking, Joan. Get a picture of your adversary before the blighter creeps up behind you. Tactical advantage and all that.

Weech He did actually give me a brief description of what we were to expect.

Edna Capital. So, what's this Clegg fellow like then?

Weech He's very average apparently. Nondescript.

Clegg enters during what follows, unseen by Edna

He stands listening and yawning. He looks tired, carries a clipboard and wears a stupid moustache. Once certain that Edna's tirade is over, he will make his presence known

Edna I might have known. They're always the worst, that sort. Jumped-up nobodies who think by virtue of the tiddly bit of authority their lowly rank affords them, they can inconvenience those of us who are really working our fingers to the bone to make a go of things. Just when we'd seen off old Adolf, a thousand mini-versions rose up out of the ranks of the civil service to ensure our lives remained a bloomin' misery. Seen one, Sam, you've seen them all. Inspectors, assessors, administrators. Thorns in the backside of this once proud nation. They'd happily bring this country to its knees with their petty bureaucratic meddlings given half a chance. Little bloomin' Hitlers! I'll tell you this for nothing, Joan, If I had my way, I'd sack the bloomin lot of them, forthwith. And believe you me, you'd find that Great Britain would run a great deal more efficiently for their passing. Why on earth we're forced to kowtow to the blighters I'll never know. There's no greater obstacle to progress than having to justify every step you take to some tiresomely officious flea-brained nonentity with a clipboard and a stupid moustache. It's as much as I can do to force myself to even give 'em the time of day, sometimes.

Clegg Good morning. The name's Clegg. Railway Inspector. I understand from Mr Blakeworth that you've been expecting me.

Edna Yes of course. Good morning. Lovely to meet you. I'm Lady Edna Chesterford. And this is Joan Weech, our extremely efficient——

Clegg Shall we get on, Lady Chesterford? It's been a very tiring day thus far.

Edna Of course, Mr Clegg. Will Mr Blakeworth not be joining us?

Clegg Mr Blakeworth has urgent business to attend to at the golf club. An extraordinary meeting of the membership committee I believe. He has, however, informed me that you are temporarily unable to utilize your best rolling stock...?

Edna Yes. We trust you'll see fit to — um——

Joan Make certain allowances——

Edna —in the circumstances.

Clegg As I am sure you'll appreciate, Lady Chesterford, the law can make no allowances. The law recognizes only facts.

Dan and Weech appear ready for the off

Edna All set, Sam? Dan?

Dan Ready as we'll ever be.

Clegg Is there a bar on board?

Edna Ah — Not as such.

Clegg Clarify?

Joan As this is a dry run, you being the only official passenger, we assumed that it wouldn't be required.

Weech We were certain you wouldn't be permitted to drink on duty, Mr Clegg.

Clegg That is indeed so. But I must inspect all facilities.

Edna The new bar is still under construction, unfortunately.
Clegg Hmm. She'll be ready for the eight forty-seven tomorrow, I presume? It's more than my job's worth to grant a licence without your firm assurance that it will be. Assuming that is the outcome of my inspection.
Edna Dan?
Dan It's impossible, ma'am. If I'm to carry out my duties here.
Edna You'll just have to go and get on with it now. I shall assume your duties as fireman. Joan – you'll have to take over as guard. Is that OK?
Joan I'll be fine, Lady Chesterford.
Weech I'm sorry, Dan. I know how much this meant to you.
Dan It can't be helped, Reverend. Though I won't say it don't hurt.
Clegg I think we've wasted enough time now. You may take the train out.

Dan exits, sadly

Joan Where would you care to sit, Mr Clegg? Back, facing or sideways?
Clegg Thank you — I will stand for the moment. To observe the departure.

Edna and Weech get the train fired up and ready to move. She judders and shakes and begins to pull out. Noise and movement

Edna This is it, Sam.
Weech I just hope that coupling holds.
Joan Good luck, Uncle! Lady Chesterford!
Clegg (*writing*) Official time of departure, twelve-o-three. Actual time of departure, twelve-o-nine.
Joan Surely we're entitled to be timed as from now?
Clegg I trust you're not telling me how best to do my job, miss?
Joan Of course not, Mr Clegg.
Weech We're on our way!

Edna rapidly becomes hot and flustered as she shovels

Come on, old girl, show us what you can do!
Edna I'm doing my best, Sam!
Weech I meant the Thunderbolt, Edna. She appears to be holding. Another fifty yards and it's downhill all the way to Ravens Wood.
Joan Everything all right with you so far, Mr Clegg?
Clegg I'd imagine you have more important things to concern yourself

with than my general well-being, miss. I am about to conduct an emergency test.

Joan Not after the delay, surely?

Clegg I am duty bound to have the brakes tested, miss. I suggest you stand by to implement correct procedure.

Clegg pulls the emergency cord. The bell rings in the guards van. Joan applies the brake. The Titfield Thunderbolt starts to separate from the carriage and move away

Weech We're over the top and she's running well. Can you feel the difference?

Joan looks out and realizes they have separated

Clegg (*writing*) Test satisfactory. You may proceed.

Clegg sits yawning in the armchair

Weech Now we'll show him.

Edna looks back

Edna Sam!

Weech looks back. Joan hastily draws the blinds/curtains in the carriage

Weech Good heavens, Edna! We've uncoupled!

Edna You'll have to put her in reverse, Sam.

Clegg What are you doing, miss?

Joan Testing the blinds, Mr Clegg, sir.

Clegg That's somewhat unorthodox, miss, at this juncture in the proceedings.

Joan No stone unturned, Mr Clegg, sir.

Edna and Weech start to reverse the train back towards the carriage

Clegg It does feel incredibly smooth, Miss. Almost like we're not moving at all.

Joan Oh but we are, Mr Clegg, we are. Now why don't you make yourself comfortable, you must be very tired after this morning's exertions on the golf course.

Clegg Do you know, miss, I think I shall. I must confess I was expecting a much rougher ride of it than this when I saw the age of your rolling stock.

Joan sets him up with a foot-stool, etc.

Joan Oh it's far more comfortable than it looks, Mr Clegg. In fact there are those who swear it's fine enough to live in, this little beauty.
Clegg I wouldn't go quite that far, miss. Though it does have a strangely homely feel about it. You may...go about your duty, miss. (*He yawns*) I shall be perfectly content here by myself.
Weech This is all very well, Edna, but without the coupling we can't tow her. We may as well just give up the ghost.
Edna There must be a way.

Clegg snores loudly and contentedly. Joan slips out of the carriage

Weech We're done for, Joan. What's Clegg to say about it?
Joan He's blissfully unaware of the problem, Uncle. He's sleeping like a baby.
Edna Then we're not quite beaten yet. In fact, that might just buy us the time we need. (*Looking off*) Because unless I'm very much mistaken, there might be one last way we can manage to save the day.
Joan I'm not with you, Lady Chesterford.
Edna Any idea where exactly we are, Joan?
Joan Well — we're somewhere near Ravens Wood, by the look of it.
Edna Quite right, Joan. And here's the young fellow might just be the answer to all our prayers.

Harry appears, shirt-sleeved and magnificent

Joan (*impressed*) Harry.
Harry I can't believe you've made an unscheduled stop just to watch a man at work, Lady C. Joan.
Edna We've got your father on board, Harry. He's under arrest.
Joan There was an accident.
Harry He's all right?
Joan He's fine.
Edna Perhaps even a reformed man. But what's more important—at the moment—is that we need to borrow your drive chain.
Harry Ground my roller, Lady C? Not on your life.
Weech You're our last hope, Harry.
Harry You don't understand. You're asking me to abandon my work, and assist in the arrest of my father to boot.

Joan He says he's ready to change his ways, Harry. For your sake.
Weech I'll vouch for him in court.
Edna And I'll persuade Blakeworth to do the same.
Weech And we'll get you another drive-chain, of course.
Edna You'd be doing Titfield an enormous service.
Joan We'd be eternally grateful, Harry.
Harry I'm not sure about this.
Joan Oh Harry. I'll do anything you ask. Absolutely anything.
Harry I don't know...
Joan I — I'll marry you tomorrow — if you'd like?
Harry You will?
Joan Uncle?
Weech You have my blessing. And I'd be at your service.
Joan You'd be conducting our service, Uncle.
Weech Quite right. That must be what I meant.
Harry Oh, Joan.
Joan Oh, Harry.

Harry and Joan snog

Weech Good God.
Edna This is all very well but——
Weech
Edna } (*together*) Not now!!

Harry and Joan reluctantly break apart

Harry (*loudly*) Stand by to connect the train!
All Shhhhhhh.
Harry Sorry. (*Softly*) Stand by to connect the train. I'll fetch the drive-chain. Then I'll come into Mallingford with you, Joan, if that's all right. In fact I don't think I'll ever let you out of my sight again. Just in case you think to change your mind.

Harry exits

Recorded music to bridge scenes. Mix with train noises as The Titfield Thunderbolt fires up, sets off and eventually steams into Mallingford. If there is the budget for an impressively constructed Titfield Thunderbolt it should not be revealed until now, when it can steam on to the stage front first. The cast can then alight from the train to perform what follows. If there is not the budget for an impressive life-size steam engine then the next scene will work perfectly well taking place on the train, as in this scene. Use smoke machines if you've got them

SCENE 7
Mallingford Station

As they arrive at Mallingford the audience are the crowd gathered along the line waving them home

Joan Look at the crowd gathered at the station!
Weech Looks like the good and the great of both Titfield and Mallingford have turned out to see us in.
Edna And not just the good and the great, Sam. Isn't that—(*Point out, name and describe humorously somebody in the audience – either invent people and occupations or put local knowledge to good use)*
Weech It is, too. And look, there's—(*Point out, name and describe humorously somebody else in the audience*)
All Hallo! Yoo-hoo!

What with all this shouting, Clegg wakes up

Clegg What's going on?
Joan We've arrived at Mallingford, Mr Clegg.
Edna Some minutes ago, sir. We didn't like to wake you.
Joan You looked so comfortable.
Clegg Just resting my eyes, miss, I assure you. Now let me see. Nine minutes late by my calculations.
Weech But we made up the three and half we were behind at the off.
Edna And we'd have been bang on time if you hadn't pulled that cord.
Joan You must allow some latitude, surely, Mr Clegg?
Clegg Facts, young lady, are facts. They cannot be argued with, I'm afraid.
Edna Then it has all been in vain. However, I would like to say, everybody, that this was a valiant attempt. We should be proud of ourselves, at least, for that. That our small, beleaguered community has shown some stickability and has stood up for itself in the face of these finickity bloomin' bureaucrats, is worthy, I feel, of note. And if defeated we must be, let us take heart from our endeavours and — in addition — accept the outcome with dignity. Now while I have your attention, I would further like to add——
Clegg If you'd stop your interminable speechifying for a moment, Lady Chesterford, I am attempting here to conclude my calculations. Now — average speed — twenty-four point two-five miles per hour. Hmm. If I may hazard a comment, I think you were particularly fortunate. All other requirements having been satisfactory, it would have been a pity if your timing had let you down.

Weech Fortunate!

Clegg In point of fact, had you reached an average speed of twenty-five miles an hour, it would have exceeded the limits imposed on a light railway. I'd advise you to be careful next time. Now, my work here appears to be done. (*Handing Edna a form*) Thank you all, and good luck for the future.

Clegg exits

Edna What's he saying?

Harry You've done it!

Weech We have?

Weech
Edna } (*together*) We've done it! We've done it!

Weech, Joan and Edna hug

Joan Congratulations, Uncle. Lady Chesterford.

They realize that Harry is excluded from the celebrations

Edna I have to say, young Crump, we couldn't have done this without you.

Weech Indeed, Harry, we're extremely grateful.

Edna In fact, if you ever get fed up with that dirty stinky old steamroller of yours, you'd be more than welcome to a job with us.

Joan On our dirty, stinky old steam engine.

Edna Oh... Quite right.

Joan I almost forgot. I'd better let Sergeant Wilson and your father out of the guard's van.

Harry Don't worry. A little bit longer won't do him any harm.

Joan I was more concerned about Sergeant Wilson.

Harry You don't have a soft spot for the Sergeant do you, by any chance?

Joan Of course not! The very idea.

Joan starts to exit

Harry Only I have heard he's rather a good-looking fellow.

Joan I can't say I've noticed, Harry.

Weech She'll do you proud, Harry, if I know that niece of mine.

Harry I'm sure of it, Mr Weech. I just hope I can prove myself worthy of her.

Weech Call me Sam, lad. We're near enough family now after all.
Edna Oh, and I'd be grateful if we could cease this Lady C business and you'd see fit to call me — Edna from now on, Harry. If I might call you Harry?
Harry Sure — Edna.
Edna Capital. Now. I have it on good authority that there are pubs in Mallingford town. Though not a patch on the old *Pig and Whistle* I'll warrant, and doubtless sadly lacking in characters of the calibre of our own Mr Valentine. But nonetheless I do feel an overwhelming urge to repair to one without further delay. Any objections?

There are none

Then the motion is carried.

They all head off towards the pub, Edna being the last to go. At the last moment she turns back, tearfully and speaks fondly to The Titfield Thunderbolt

Edna Well done, old girl. Well done.

The Titfield Thunderbolt responds with a joyful whistle

The cast enter to sing The Ferroequinologist's Lament № 6. (*Reprise*)

All And as she rolls across the night
That ghost train makes the grade,
Through Campion and Cotton-grass
Where once were sleepers laid.
Via Bryony and Bedstraw,
Thyme and Traveller's Joy,
Through Rosebay and Meadowsweet,
Balsam and Bilberry,
Whistling eternally,
Titfield for Mallingford – Ahoy!

CURTAIN

FURNITURE AND PROPERTY LIST

Further dressing may be added at the director's discretion

ACT I

Scene 1

No props required

Scene 2

On stage: Titfield Railway Station
Wall calendar showing the date Friday 6th June, 1952

Off stage: Sack (**Dan**)
Poster which says: "*Important Notice. The passenger train service between Titfield station and Mallingford Junction will be permanently withdrawn on and from Saturday, the 21st June, 1952, and accordingly the public is hereby given notice of closure.*" (**Clifton**)

Personal: **Clifton**: watch
Blakeworth: cycle clip, watch
Dan: watch
Vernon: watch
Crump: watch

Scene 3

Off stage: Steering wheel (**Edna**)
Steering wheel (**Harry**)

Scene 4

On stage: Titfield Railway Station
Wall calendar showing the date Friday 6th June, 1952

Off stage: Poster which says: "*Very Important Notice. An alternative passenger Omnibus Service will be operated by Crump and Son Road Transport Company (incorporating the Titfield Road Transport Company) servicing the area formerly covered by the railway* (**Vernon**)
Photograph (**Vernon**)

Personal: **Clifton**: watch, whistle

SCENE 5

On stage: THE VICARAGE
Picture on the wall of The Titfield Thunderbolt

Personal: **Weech**: railway magazine, bible

SCENE 6

On stage: THE *PIG AND WHISTLE* PUBLIC HOUSE
Set: A public bar
A glass of sherry

Personal: **Valentine**: large glass of gin

SCENE 7

On stage: TITFIELD RAILWAY STATION
Wall calendar showing the date Friday 13th June, 1952

Off stage: Poster which says: "*Titfield-Mallingford Railway, Ministry of Transport, inquiry will be held at the Village Hall, Titfield, Friday 13th June*" (**Clifton**)
Newspaper (**Weech**)
Sticker proclaiming: "*It's safer by bus*" (**Vernon**)
Briefcase (**Ruddock**)

SCENE 8

On stage: THE VILLAGE HALL

Personal: **Vernon**: sheet of paper with a speech written on it, envelope of money

SCENE 9

On stage: TITFIELD RAILWAY STATION
Wall calendar showing the date Monday 16th June, 1952

Off stage: Huge chain (**Harry**)

Personal: **Mrs Bottomley**: formidable handbag

ACT II

Scene 1

Personal: **Harry**: torch
Vernon: torch, shotgun

Scene 2

Off stage: Assorted containers eg: fire bucket, army helmet, Valentine's tankard, ice bucket, empty gin bottle, saucepan, tea-pot, vase, bed pan or a potty, Mrs Bottomley's handbag, beer barrel Mr Blakeworth's hat, etc. (**All**)

Personal: **Dan**: sack
Joan: watch
Valentine: hip flask. *In it*: liquid

Scene 3

On stage: The *Pig and Whistle* Public House
A public bar

Scene 4

On stage: Near the Engine Shed

Off stage: Pick-axe, torch (**Vernon**)
Torch (**Blakeworth**)
Torch (**Harry**)
Torch (**Sergeant Wilson**)

Scene 5

On stage: The Vicarage
Picture on the wall of The Titfield Thunderbolt (*removable*)

Scene 6

On stage: Titfield Railway Station
Wall calendar showing the date Monday 14th July, 1952
On stage: Dan's Carriage Home
Old, threadbare armchair
Cushions
Curtains
Standard lamp

Foot stool
Emergency Cord } *Pre-set in train area*
Shovel (**Edna**)

Off stage: Steam train

Personal: **Clegg**: clipboard and pen, stupid moustache

SCENE 7

On stage: MALLINGFORD RAILWAY STATION/DAN'S CARRIAGE HOME

Personal: **Clegg**: form

LIGHTING PLOT

Property fittings required: nil
Various interior and exterior settings

ACT I, Scene 1

To open: Bright general lighting

Cue 1	**Edna** (*introducing the cast*) "Starring..." *Light each character as they briefly step forward and strike a pose*	(Page 2)

ACT I, Scene 2

To open: Bright general interior lighting

No cues

ACT I, Scene 3

To open: Bright general exterior lighting

Cue 2	**Harry Crump** enters the auditorium on his Steamroller followed by **Lady Edna Chesterford** in her Morris Minor *Follow spots or some auditorium lighting fade on their exit*	(Page 5)

ACT I, Scene 4

To open: Bright general lighting

No cues

ACT I, Scene 5

No cues

To open: Bright general house interior lighting

No cues

ACT I, Scene 6

To open: Bright general pub interior lighting

No cues

ACT I, Scene 7

To open: Bright general interior lighting

No cues

ACT I, Scene 8

To open: Bright general interior lighting

Cue 3 **Vernon, Coggett, Edna and Blakeworth** join the audience (Page 20)
Moderate auditorium lighting

ACT I, Scene 9

To open: Bright general interior lighting

Cue 4 **Edna** "Tunnel coming up" (Page 27)
Black-out for a few moments then resume previous lighting

ACT II, Scene 1

To open: Night-time darkness

No cues

ACT II, Scene 2

To open: Lights up in auditorium

Cue 5 **Joan** "Tunnel coming up" (Page 34)
Black-out for a few moments then resume previous lighting

Cue 6 **Edna** "...I shall buy you a drink at *The Pig and Whistle*" (Page 37)
Fade to black-out

ACT II, SCENE 3

To open: Bright general pub interior lighting

No cues

ACT II, SCENE 4

To open: Night-time darkness

No cues

ACT II, SCENE 5

No cues

To open: Bright general house interior lighting

ACT II, SCENE 6

No cues

To open: Bright general interior lighting

EFFECTS PLOT

ACT I

Cue 1	**Edna**: "Ladies and gentlemen..." *Early radio play style music under*	(Page 2)
Cue 2	**Edna**: "... the Titfield Thunderbolt!" *Music stops*	(Page 2)
Cue 3	The train comes in *Sound effect of a steam train arriving (Optional)*	(Page 3)
Cue 4	**Edna**: "... Mungo's Farmyard" *Sound effect of squawking chickens and miscellaneous farm animals (Optional)*	(Page 5)
Cue 5	**Joan**: "Yes, Uncle." *A doorbell rings*	(Page 9)
Cue 6	**Weech**: "Alleluia!" *Scene change music, something that heralds the arrival of a new positivism*	(Page 17)
Cue 7	**Clifton**: sticks a notice on the wall *Ominously sounding bell toll*	(Page 17)
Cue 8	**Edna, Weech** and **Vernon**: "It's safer by bus!" *Scene change music*	(Page 24)
Cue 9	**Edna**: "Tunnel coming up." *Train whistle*	(Page 27)
Cue 10	**Harry**: "God I love that woman." *Horrendous scraping, metallic, destructive noise (Optional)*	(Page 31)
Cue 11	**Joan**: "... rest of our journey." *Sound effect of a steam train fading away*	(Page 32)

ACT II

Cue 12	**Harry** and **Vernon** enter *Sounds of owls and other night-time creatures (Optional)*	(Page 33)

Cue 13	**Vernon** fires a gun *Sound of a gun-shot and water splashes down on* **Harry**	(Page 34)
Cue 14	**Joan**: "Tunnel coming up." *Sounds of whistles and other noises continue*	(Page 34)
Cue 15	**Edna** opens the window *Train noises increase in volume*	(Page 34)
Cue 16	**Edna** closes the window *Reduce volume of train noises*	(Page 35)
Cue 17	**Edna**: "... Mum's the word." *'Busy' instrumental music played low under the action*	(Page 37)
Cue 18	To open Scene 4 *Night noises (Optional)*	(Page 40)
Cue 19	**Blakeworth**: "... straight for the river!" *Sound effect of a steam train crashing into a river with water splashing on* **Blakeworth** *and the* **Audience**	(Page 42)
Cue 20	**Joan**: "... Don't lose faith." *Doorbell*	(Page 44)
Cue 21	The train begins to pull out *Train noise and movement (Optional)*	(Page 51)
Cue 22	**Clegg** pulls the emergency cord *Bell rings*	(Page 52)
Cue 23	**Harry** exits *Recorded music to bridge scenes. Mix with train noises as the Titfield Thunderbolt fires up, sets off and eventually steams into Mallingford - use smoke machines for steam effect*	(Page 54)
Cue 24	**Edna**: "Well done, old girl, well done." *Joyful train whistle*	(Page 57)

Lightning Source UK Ltd.
Milton Keynes UK
UKOW06f1625060915

258135UK00011B/239/P